The World Around Us

Geography Projects and Activities

by Denise Bieniek, M.S.
Illustrated by Wayne Becker

Copyright © 1996 by Troll Communications L.L.C. All rights reserved. Permission is hereby granted to the purchaser to reproduce these pages, in sufficient quantities to meet yearly student needs, for use in the buyer's classroom. All other permissions must be obtained from the publisher.

Troll CREATIVE TEACHER IDEAS

Troll Creative Teacher Ideas was designed to help today's dedicated, time-pressured teacher. Created by teachers for teachers, this innovative series provides a wealth of classroom ideas to help reinforce important concepts and stimulate your students' creative thinking skills.

Each book in the series focuses on a different curriculum theme to give you the flexibility to teach any given skill at any time of the year. The wide range of ideas and activities included in each book are certain to help you create an atmosphere where students are continually eager to learn new concepts and develop important skills.

We hope this comprehensive series will provide you with everything you need to foster a fun and challenging learning environment for your students. **Troll Creative Teacher Ideas** is a resource you'll turn to again and again!

Titles in this series:

Classroom Decor:
Decorate Your Classroom from Bulletin Boards to Time Lines

Creative Projects: Quick and Easy Art Projects

Earth Alert: Environmental Studies for Grades 4-6

Explore the World: Social Studies Projects and Activities

Healthy Bodies, Healthy Minds

Holidays Around the World: Multicultural Projects and Activities

It All Adds Up: Math Skill-Building Activities for Grades 4-6

Learning Through Literature:
Projects and Activities for Linking Literature and Writing

Story Writing: Creative Writing Projects and Activities

Think About It: Skill-Building Puzzles Across the Curriculum

The World Around Us: Geography Projects and Activities

World Explorers: Discover the Past

Metric Conversion Chart

1 inch = 2.54 cm	1 foot = .305 m	1 yard = .914 m
1 mile = 1.61 km	1 fluid ounce = 29.573 ml	1 cup = .24 l
1 pint = .473 l	1 teaspoon = 4.93 ml	1 tablespoon = 14.78 ml

Contents

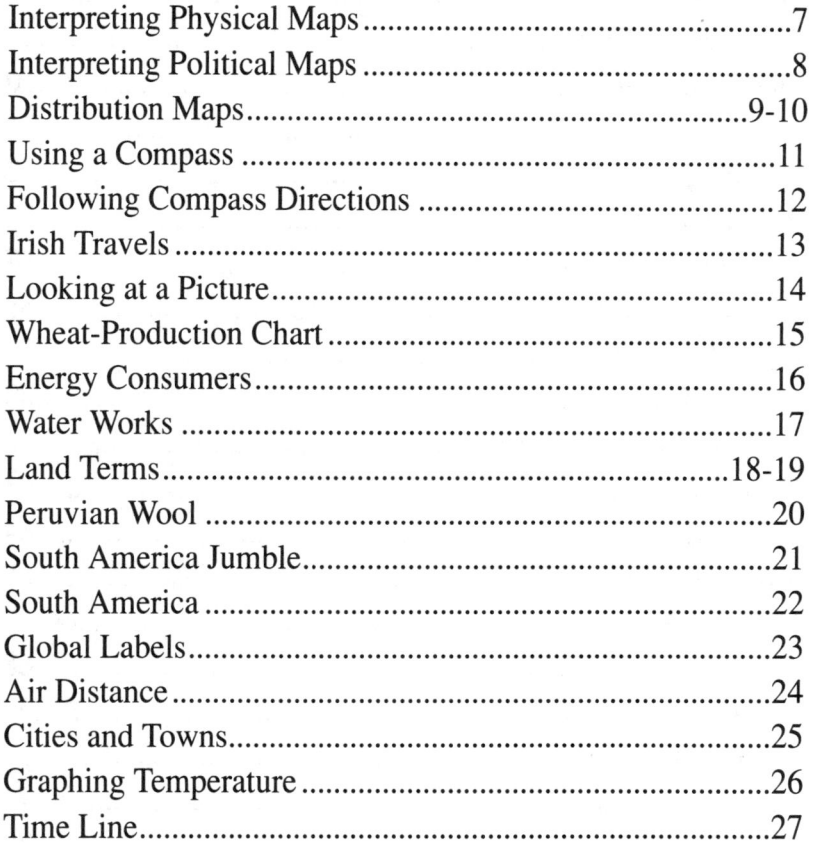

Map Symbols	5
Mapping Mania	6
Interpreting Physical Maps	7
Interpreting Political Maps	8
Distribution Maps	9-10
Using a Compass	11
Following Compass Directions	12
Irish Travels	13
Looking at a Picture	14
Wheat-Production Chart	15
Energy Consumers	16
Water Works	17
Land Terms	18-19
Peruvian Wool	20
South America Jumble	21
South America	22
Global Labels	23
Air Distance	24
Cities and Towns	25
Graphing Temperature	26
Time Line	27
Surface and Population	28-29
Model Elevations	30
Race Against Time	31
Map Outlines	32
Geography Picture File	33
Lost City of Atlantis	34
Games from Afar	35
Geographical Interactive Poster	36
Geography Bulletin Board	37
States Word Search	38
World Map Jigsaw Puzzle	39-40
Sopaipillas Recipe	41
Fiesta Eggs	42
Descriptive Words	43

© 1996 Troll Creative Teacher Ideas

Through the Rain Forest	44
Abbreviated States	45
Places Puzzles	46
Statistics Pie	47
What's Wrong Here?	48
Worldwide Words	49
Finding the Similarities	50
Match Idioms	51
Culture Crossword Puzzle	52
World Travelers	53-56
Where in the World Is It?	57
World-Famous Explorers	58
Shortest Routes	59
Worldly Chitchat	60
Ecosystems of the World	61-62
Historical Clues	63
Topographical Test	64
Mountain Madness	65
Muddled Maps	66-67
City Slickers	68
Capital Concentration	69
Current Happenings	70
Let's Play "Geography"!	71
Population Scramble	72
Rivers of the World	73-74
Climate Mural Map	75
Climate Clues	76
Wonders of the World	77
Language Lessons	78
Changing Currency	79
Best Books About Geography	80
Animals Around the World	81
Class Cookbook	82
Geographical Homes	83
U.S. Landmarks Game	84-87
Geographical Glossary	88-89

© 1996 Troll Creative Teacher Ideas

Map Symbols

Name _____

Identify the symbols on the map. Then fill in the name of each symbol in the blank space next to it.

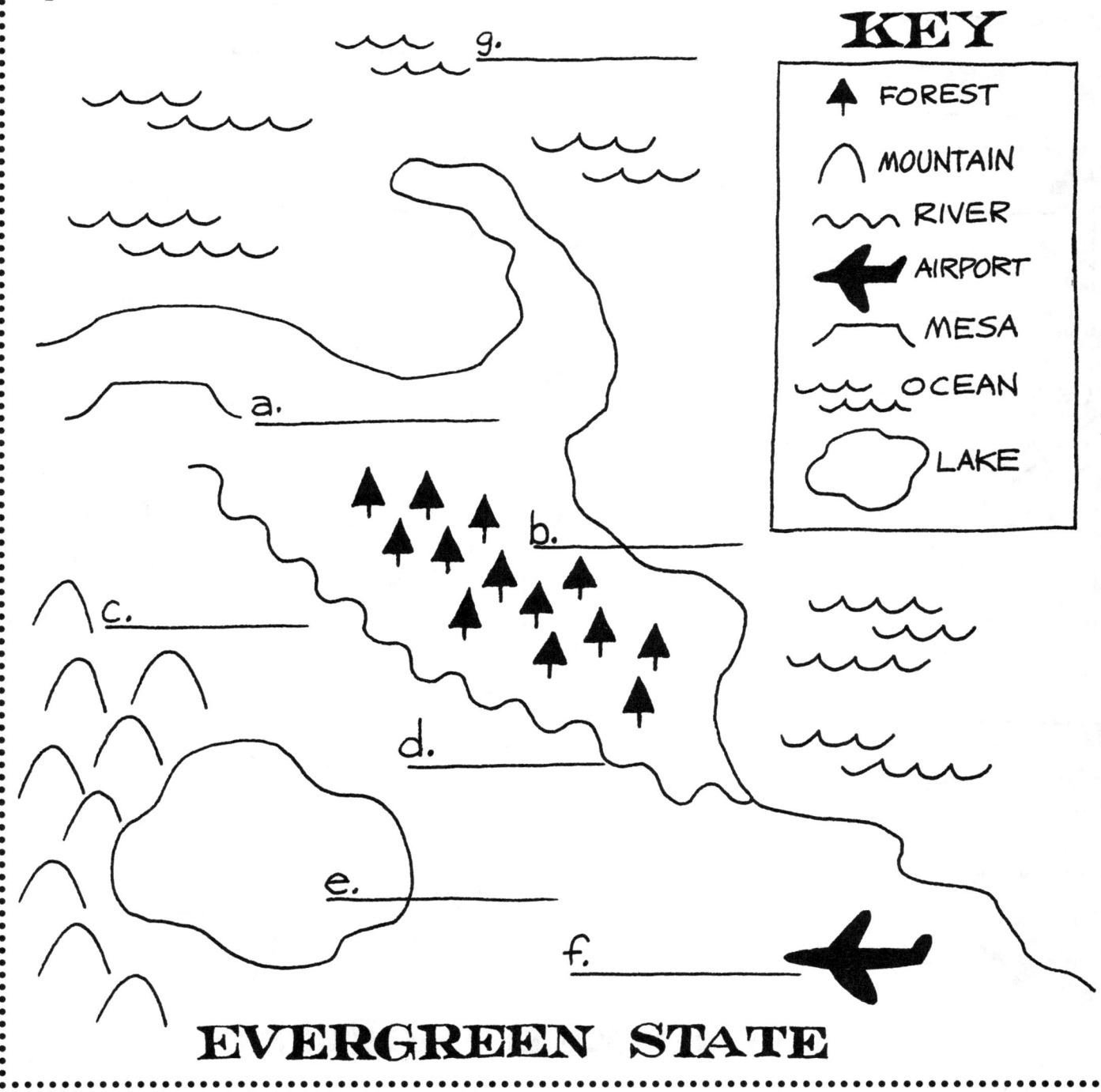

KEY
- ▲ FOREST
- ⋀ MOUNTAIN
- ∼ RIVER
- ✈ AIRPORT
- ⎯ MESA
- ≈ OCEAN
- ◯ LAKE

g. _____

a. _____

c. _____

b. _____

d. _____

e. _____

f. _____

EVERGREEN STATE

© 1996 Troll Creative Teacher Ideas

Mapping Mania

Name _____

Match each place or thing shown on the map to the corresponding picture in the key below. Write the letters of the matching pictures on the lines provided.

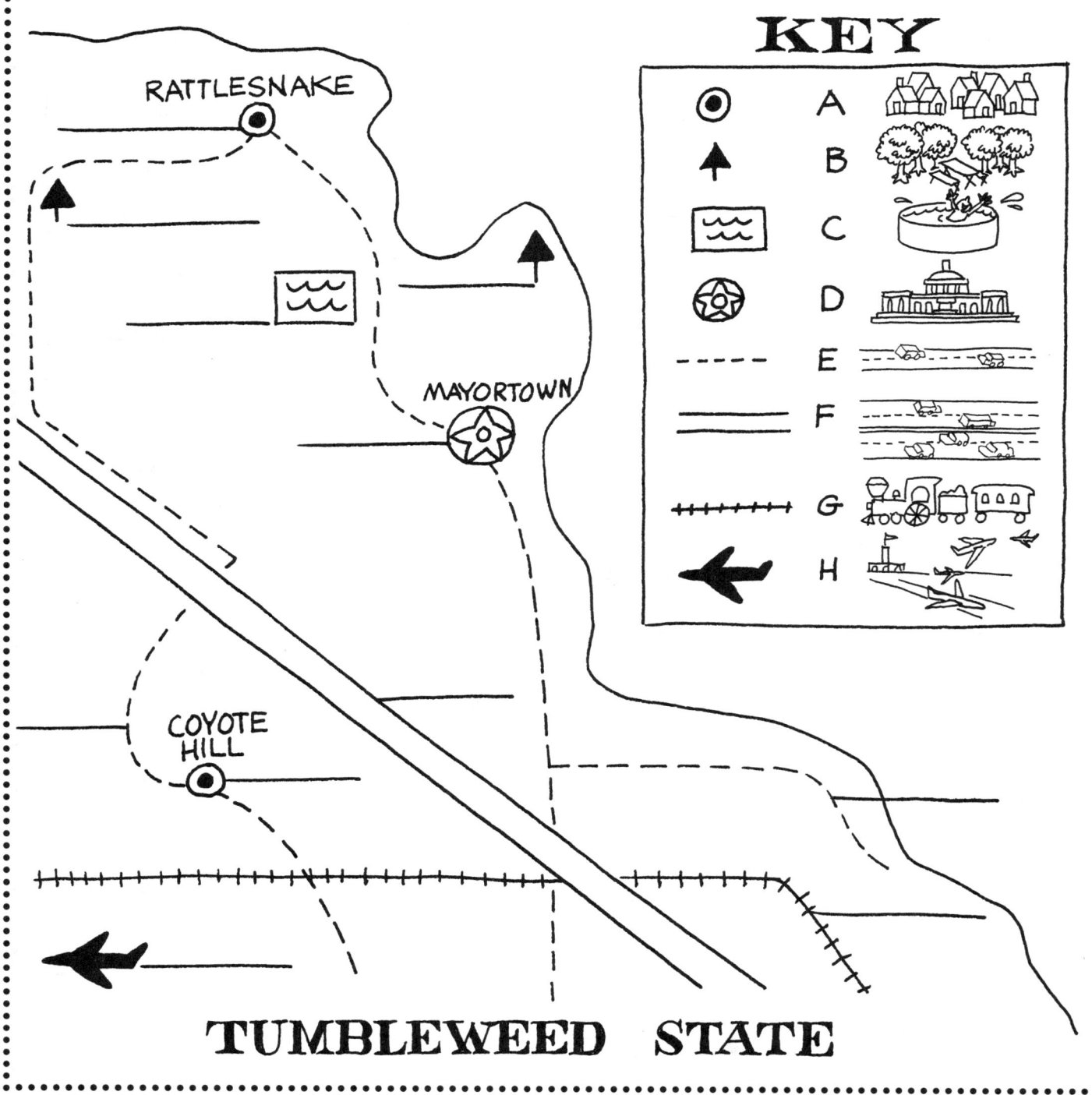

KEY

- ⊙ A
- ▲ B
- 〰️ C
- ✪ D
- - - - E
- ──── F
- ++++ G
- ✈ H

RATTLESNAKE

MAYORTOWN

COYOTE HILL

TUMBLEWEED STATE

© 1996 Troll Creative Teacher Ideas

Interpreting Physical Maps

Name _____

Answer the questions below based on information given in the map.

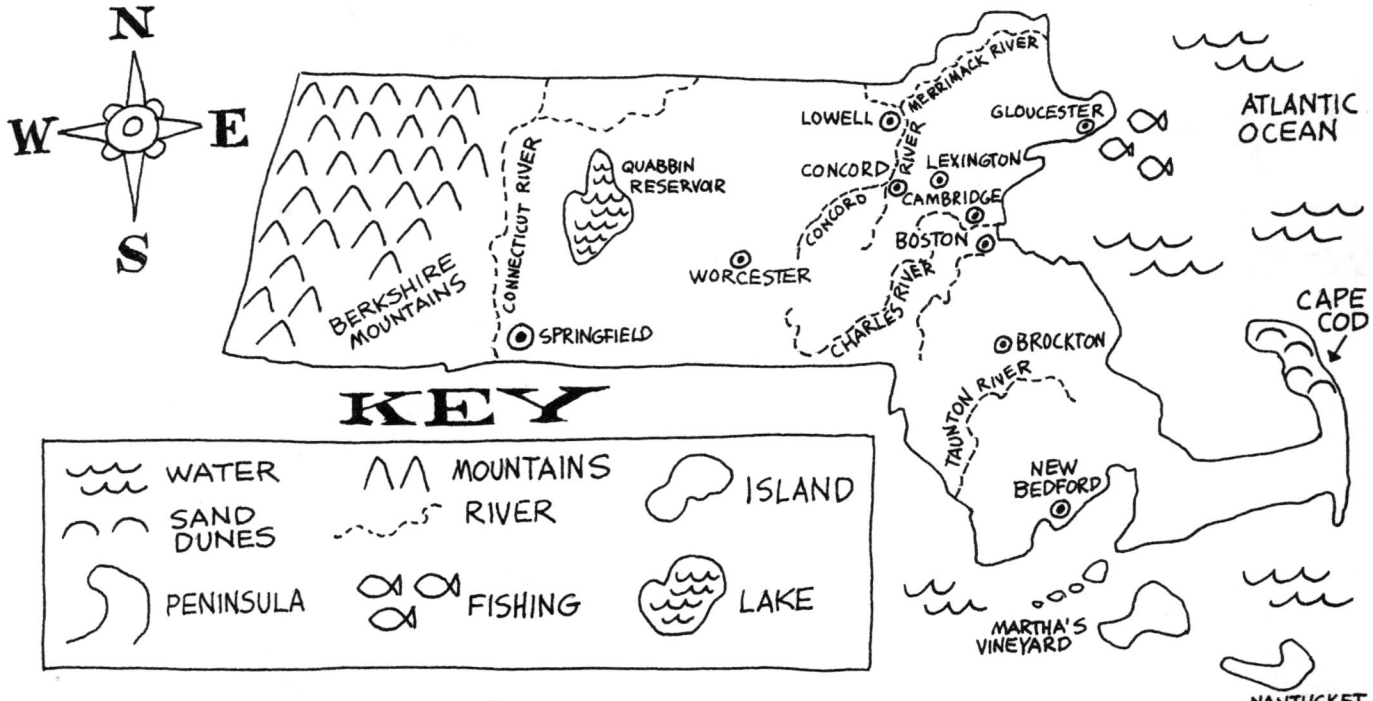

KEY
- ~~ WATER
- ⌢⌢ SAND DUNES
- ⌒ PENINSULA
- ∧∧ MOUNTAINS
- ⋯ RIVER
- 🐟🐟 FISHING
- ◯ ISLAND
- 〰 LAKE

1. If you wanted to drive to Lowell from Springfield, in which direction would you travel? _____

2. What is the name of the river that feeds into the Concord River? _____

3. Identify the peninsula to the east of Brockton. _____

4. Where in the state are the Berkshires located? _____

5. Name the ocean that runs along the coast of Massachusetts. _____

6. An island is land that is smaller than a continent and surrounded by water. Are there any islands near Massachusetts and if so, what are their names? _____

7. Are there any deserts in Massachusetts and if so, what are their names? _____

© 1996 Troll Creative Teacher Ideas

Interpreting Political Maps

Name _____

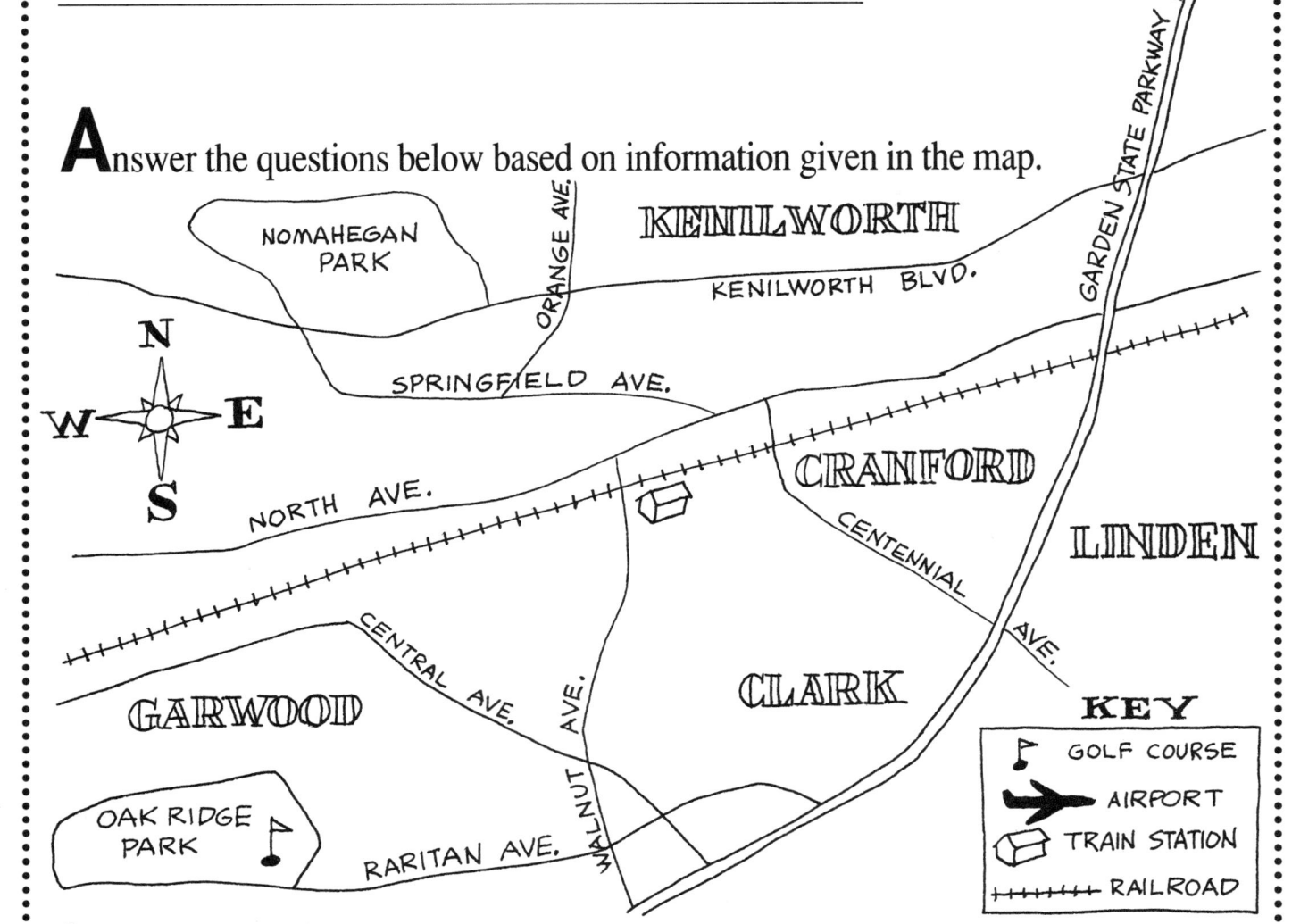

Answer the questions below based on information given in the map.

KEY
- 🏌 GOLF COURSE
- ✈ AIRPORT
- 🏠 TRAIN STATION
- ++++ RAILROAD

1. If you lived on Walnut Avenue, how might you go to reach Nomahegan Park? _____
   _____

2. What towns does the railroad run through? _____

3. Can you get onto the Garden State Parkway if you are driving west along Central Avenue? _____

4. In which direction would you be traveling if you lived in Linden and wanted to visit a friend living in Kenilworth? _____

5. Where is the airport located? _____

6. Where would you go to play golf? _____

7. Where is the train station in Cranford located? _____

© 1996 Troll Creative Teacher Ideas

Distribution Maps

Name _____

Answer the questions below based on the information given in the chart below and the map on page 10.

Traffic at U.S. Airports in 1991

Chicago (O'Hare)	59,852,330
Dallas/Fort Worth	48,198,208
Los Angeles	45,668,204
Atlanta	37,916,024
San Francisco	31,774,845
Denver	28,285,189
New York (JFK)	27,441,937
Miami	26,591,415
Newark	23,055,537
Phoenix	22,140,437
Boston	21,547,026
Detroit	21,309,046
Minneapolis/St. Paul	20,601,177
New York (LGA)	20,545,060
Las Vegas	20,171,557

1. On the map, write in the name of each airport and number of flights in and out on the blank lines next to the airport symbols. _____

2. Which airport has the most traffic? _____

3. If you were taking a flight to Los Angeles from Miami, in which direction would you be traveling? _____

4. Which state's combined airport traffic adds up to 47,986,997 flights? _____
   _____

5. How many more flights were there at Denver than Boston? _____

© 1996 Troll Creative Teacher Ideas

Distribution Maps

Name _____

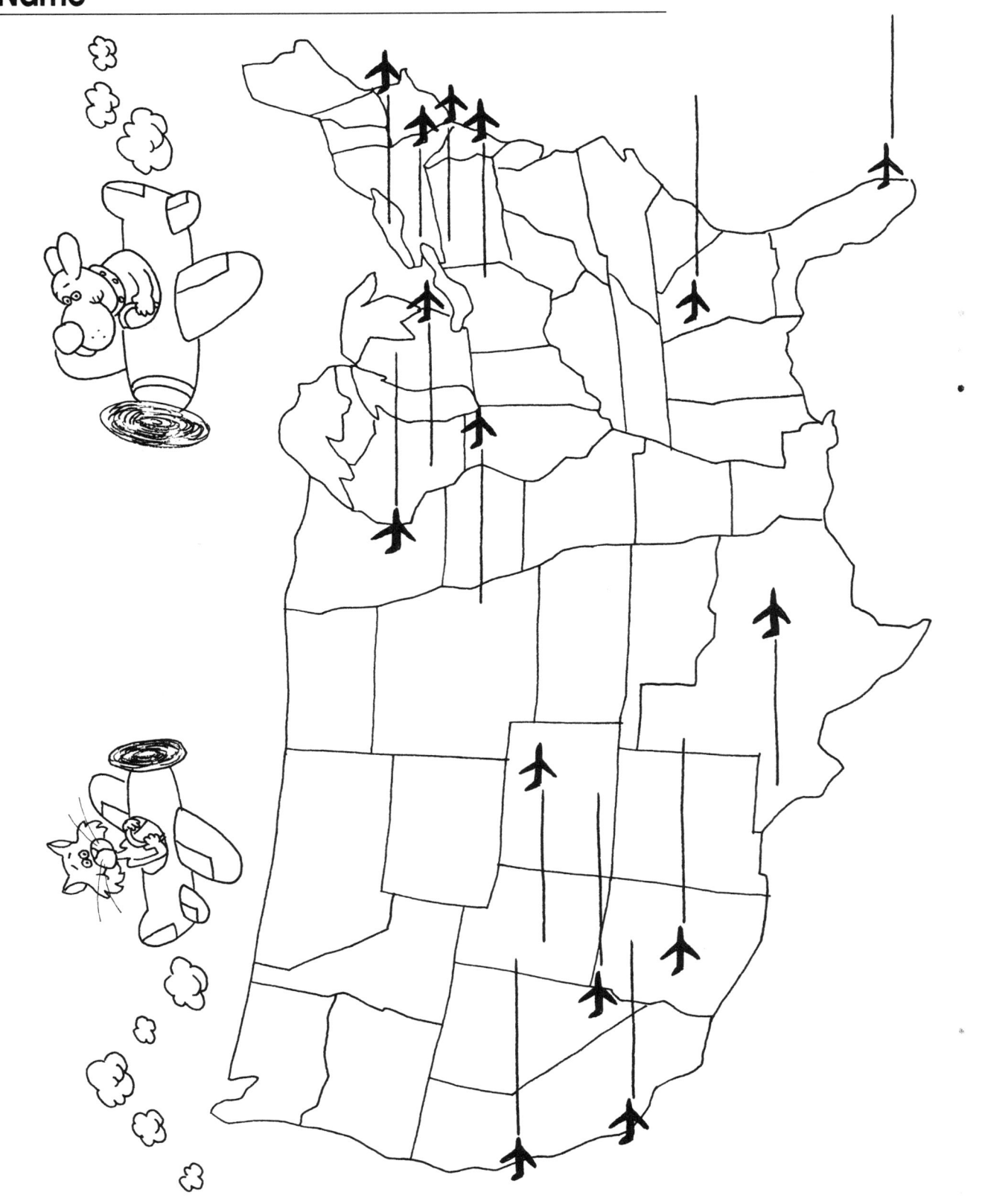

Using a Compass

Divide the class into groups of four and give each group a compass. Tell one person in each group to hold the compass. Students should then take turns as activities change.

Ask the groups to turn around slowly until their compass needles are pointing north. Give students a minute to check whether all the groups are facing the same way. Explain to the class that on a map true North is in the direction of the North Pole, but the needles in the compasses are attracted to the magnetic North, which is located south of the North Pole. Tell students that the position of this magnetic field shifts every year, so the angle between true North and the magnetic North changes slightly every year. The angle is called the declination.

Ask the groups to predict in which direction they would be facing if they turned and faced the opposite direction (south). Invite the groups to turn the opposite way and check their answers. Then make predictions for turning to their left and right.

Encourage groups to experiment with their compasses to discover which wall faces in which direction. Then write the compass directions on pieces of paper and tape them to the walls of the room in the correct positions.

Once the room is marked, you may wish to play a variation on the game "Simon Says." Use directional instructions when leading the game, such as "Point your foot south" and "Walk three paces northeast."

© 1996 Troll Creative Teacher Ideas

Following Compass Directions

Name _____

Answer the questions below based on the information given in the map.

1. You live in Nova Scotia and plan to meet some friends in Montreal. In which direction will you be traveling to meet them? _____

2. If you were hiking in the Rocky Mountains and then decided to go to Ontario, in which direction would you be traveling? _____

3. Name a province that is on the southwest side of Hudson Bay. _____

4. Which province is located east of Alberta? _____

5. Identify the province located north of Washington state. _____
_____

6. If you traveled from Baffin Island to Newfoundland, in which direction would you be going?
_____

© 1996 Troll Creative Teacher Ideas

Irish Travels

Name _____

Answer the questions based on the map of Ireland.

1. If you landed in Dublin and were going to Galway to visit relatives, approximately how far would you have to travel? _____

2. Could you reach Skibbereen from Ballyshannon in two hours going 50 miles per hour? _____

3. If you were traveling to Wexford, which airport would place you the closest: Dublin, Cork, or Shannon? _____

4. How long would it take to travel from Galway to Athlone in a train going 60 miles per hour? _____

5. Approximately how many miles from Galway is the Aran island of Inisheer? _____

6. Identify the town located between Sligo and Galway. _____

© 1996 Troll Creative Teacher Ideas

Looking at a Picture

Name _____

Look at this picture of a desert home carefully. Then answer the questions based on the information in the picture.

1. Name at least ten things you see in the picture. _____
   _____

2. Which things are made by nature? _____

3. Which things are made by people? _____

4. What do you see in the picture that indicates the type of weather that might be occurring? _____

5. In which direction are the mountains located in the picture? _____

6. This house is made of adobe brick and is only one story high. Why do you think this type of home might be good for the desert climate? _____
   _____

© 1996 Troll Creative Teacher Ideas

Wheat-Production Chart

Name _____

Answer the questions based on the information given in the chart.

SOVIET UNION

CHINA

UNITED STATES

INDIA

FRANCE

CANADA

WHEAT PRODUCTION 1990
1 SHEAF = 10,000 METRIC TONS
1 STALK = 1,000 METRIC TONS
(ROUNDED TO NEAREST 10,000)

1. How much does each sheaf of wheat symbol equal? Each individual stalk symbol? _____

2. Which country produced the most wheat in 1990? _____

3. How many more metric tons of wheat were produced by the Soviet Union than by Canada? _____

4. Which two countries had a combined tonnage equal to that of just one other country in the chart? What is the name of the country whose tonnage is equal to these two? _____

5. Suppose France had produced 45,000 metric tons of wheat. How many more sheafs would need to be added to France's line in the chart? _____

6. What was the approximate percentage of wheat produced by India compared to the Soviet Union? _____ What was the approximate percentage of wheat produced by the United States compared to the Soviet Union? _____

© 1996 Troll Creative Teacher Ideas

Energy Consumers

Name _____

Energy consumption by a country is based on its use of petroleum, natural gas, coal, hydroelectricity, and nuclear energy.

Look at the chart below carefully. Then answer the questions based on the information given in the chart.

CONSUMERS OF PRIMARY ENERGY - 1990

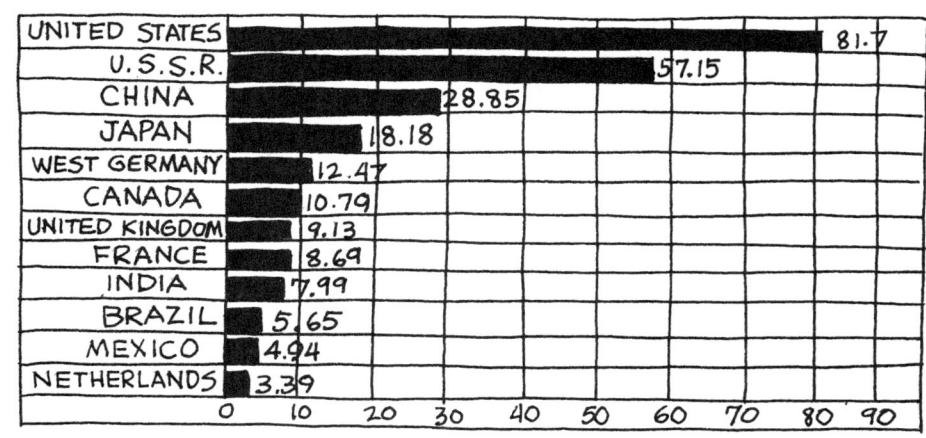

Country	Quadrillion BTU
UNITED STATES	81.7
U.S.S.R.	57.15
CHINA	28.85
JAPAN	18.18
WEST GERMANY	12.47
CANADA	10.79
UNITED KINGDOM	9.13
FRANCE	8.69
INDIA	7.99
BRAZIL	5.65
MEXICO	4.94
NETHERLANDS	3.39

1. In which country was the most energy used in 1990? The least? _____

2. How much less energy was consumed in Mexico than in China? _____

3. Which two countries' energy consumption almost equaled that of France? _____

4. What might be some reasons justifying the consumption of large amounts of energy by some countries? _____

5. What is the ratio of energy use in Brazil compared to Canada? _____

6. If West Germany had consumed 5.71 quadrillion Btus more, what would its total consumption have been? _____

   What other country would it have equaled in energy consumption? _____

© 1996 Troll Creative Teacher Ideas

Water Works

Name _____

Fill in the answers to the clues about different bodies of water to complete the crossword puzzle.

Across
4. A stream or small river that flows into another river or stream.
8. A large, moving body of fresh water that starts at a source in higher land and moves to lower land as it flows toward its mouth.
9. A deep, narrow inlet of the sea, between high, steep cliffs.
10. The great body of salt water that covers approximately 71% of Earth's surface.
12. A sheltered body of water where ships anchor and are safe from winds and storms at sea.

Down
1. A large body of salt water, much smaller than an ocean, nearly or partly surrounded by land.
2. A passageway of water that connects two large bodies of water.
3. A large area of the ocean or sea that lies within a curved coastline.
5. A small strip of water that reaches from a sea or lake into the shore land.
6. A natural or artificial lake or pond in which water is collected and stored for use.
7. A basin of shallow water linked to the sea by an inlet.
11. A body of water, usually fresh, that is surrounded by land.
13. A place in a desert where people, plants, and animals can get water, fed by underground springs or from irrigation.

© 1996 Troll Creative Teacher Ideas

Land Terms

Name _____

Read the land terms described in the glossary below. Then write the land term that matches each picture in the blank spaces.

Glossary

archipelago—group of islands
canyon—a deep, narrow valley having high, steep sides or cliffs
cape—a narrow part of land that sticks out into water along a shore
delta—land built up by soil that drops from a river at its mouth, the place where it meets a larger body of water
desert—a large land area in which there is little or no rainfall
island—land that is completely surrounded by water and is smaller than a continent
isthmus—a narrow piece of land that joins two larger bodies of land
mountain—land that rises very high, much higher than the land at its base
peninsula—a land area almost surrounded by water with a narrow link to a larger land area
plain—large, mostly flat land area
plateau—large land area that is high and generally very flat
valley—lower land between hills or mountains

© 1996 Troll Creative Teacher Ideas

Land Terms

Name _____

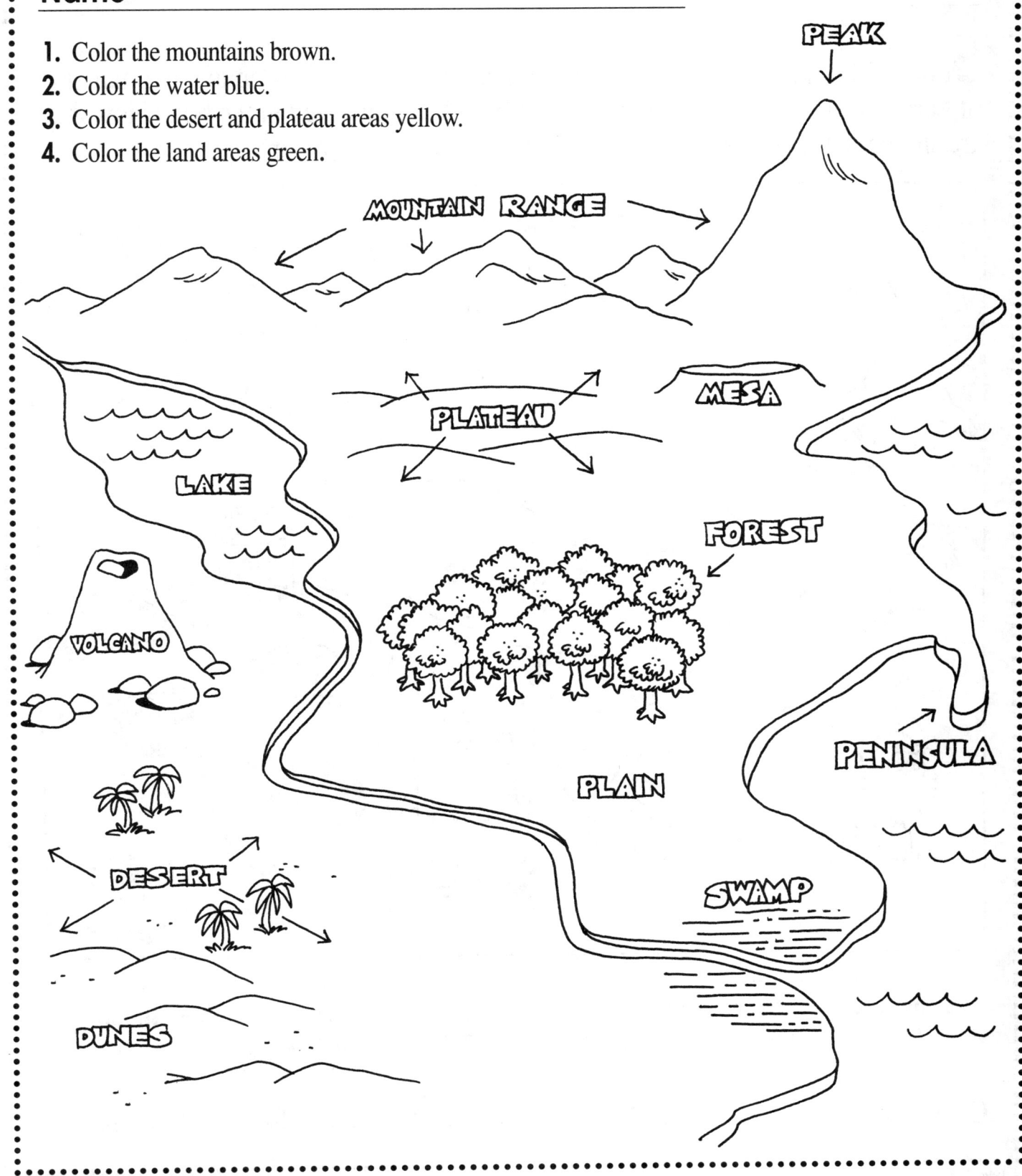

1. Color the mountains brown.
2. Color the water blue.
3. Color the desert and plateau areas yellow.
4. Color the land areas green.

PEAK

MOUNTAIN RANGE

MESA

PLATEAU

LAKE

FOREST

VOLCANO

PENINSULA

PLAIN

DESERT

SWAMP

DUNES

© 1996 Troll Creative Teacher Ideas

Peruvian Wool

Name _____

Some of the finest wool in the world comes from flocks of sheep in the mountains of Peru. Look at the scene below. Try to find the items listed in the box below that are shown in the picture. Circle the items, then color the picture.

shepherd's crook	shepherd dog	sweater	loom	shorn sheep
yarn and spindle	shearing scissors	coat	blanket	wolf

On a separate piece of paper, tell how a wool sweater is made from start to finish.

© 1996 Troll Creative Teacher Ideas

South America Jumble

Name _____

Unscramble the names of the South American countries below and write them on the lines provided. Then fill in each country's name in the correct place on the map of South America on page 22.

1. ALZEVNEEU _____
2. MOLACIOB _____
3. YANAGU _____
4. ESIRUMAN _____
5. CHRENF UIGANA _____
6. DORAUCE _____
7. REPU _____
8. ZARBIL _____
9. VILABOI _____
10. HILCE _____
11. GRANETANI _____
12. PRAUGYAA _____
13. GAURUYU _____

© 1996 Troll Creative Teacher Ideas

South America

Name _____

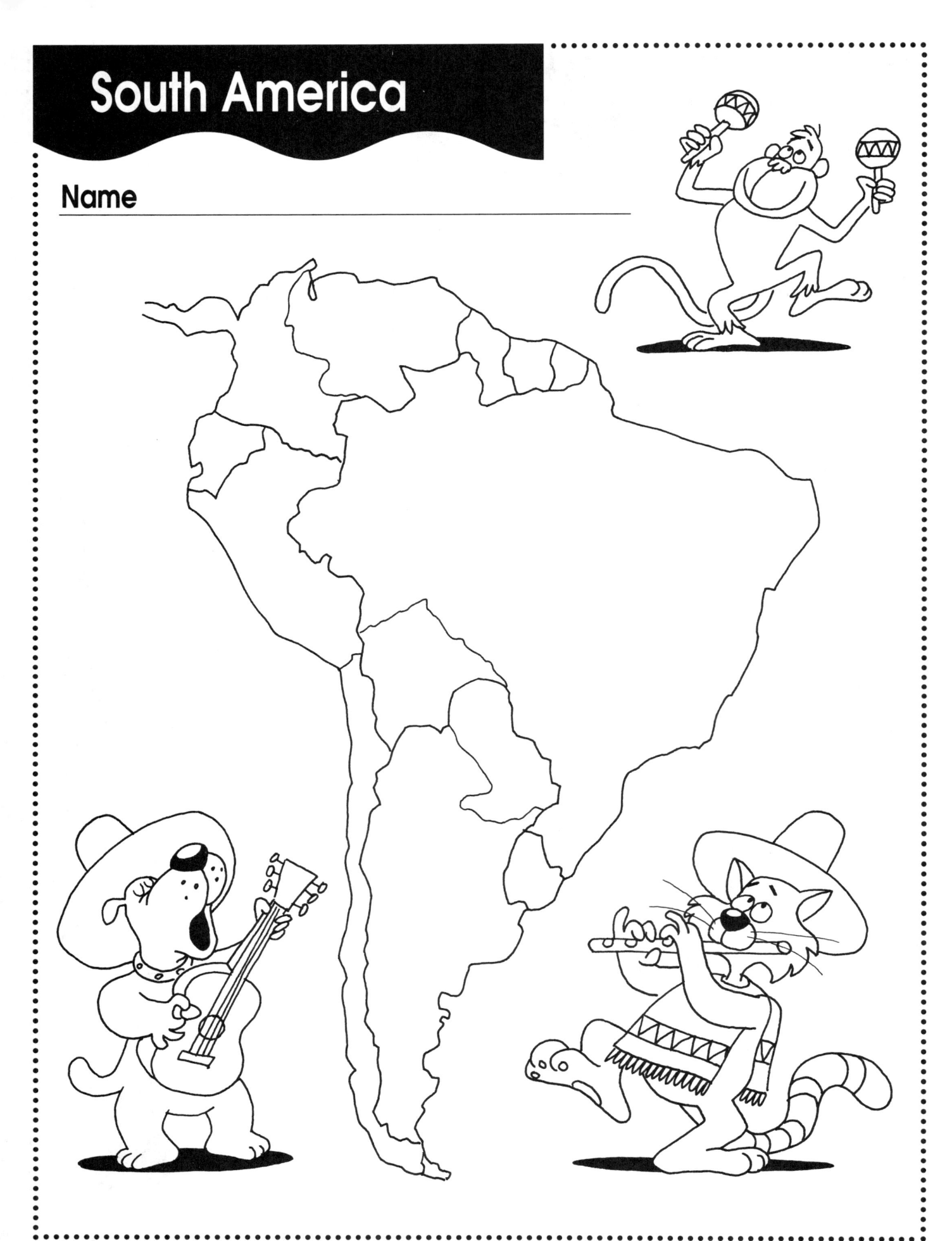

Global Labels

Name _____

Read the words in the box at the bottom of this page. Then write the appropriate label in each box in the picture of Earth.

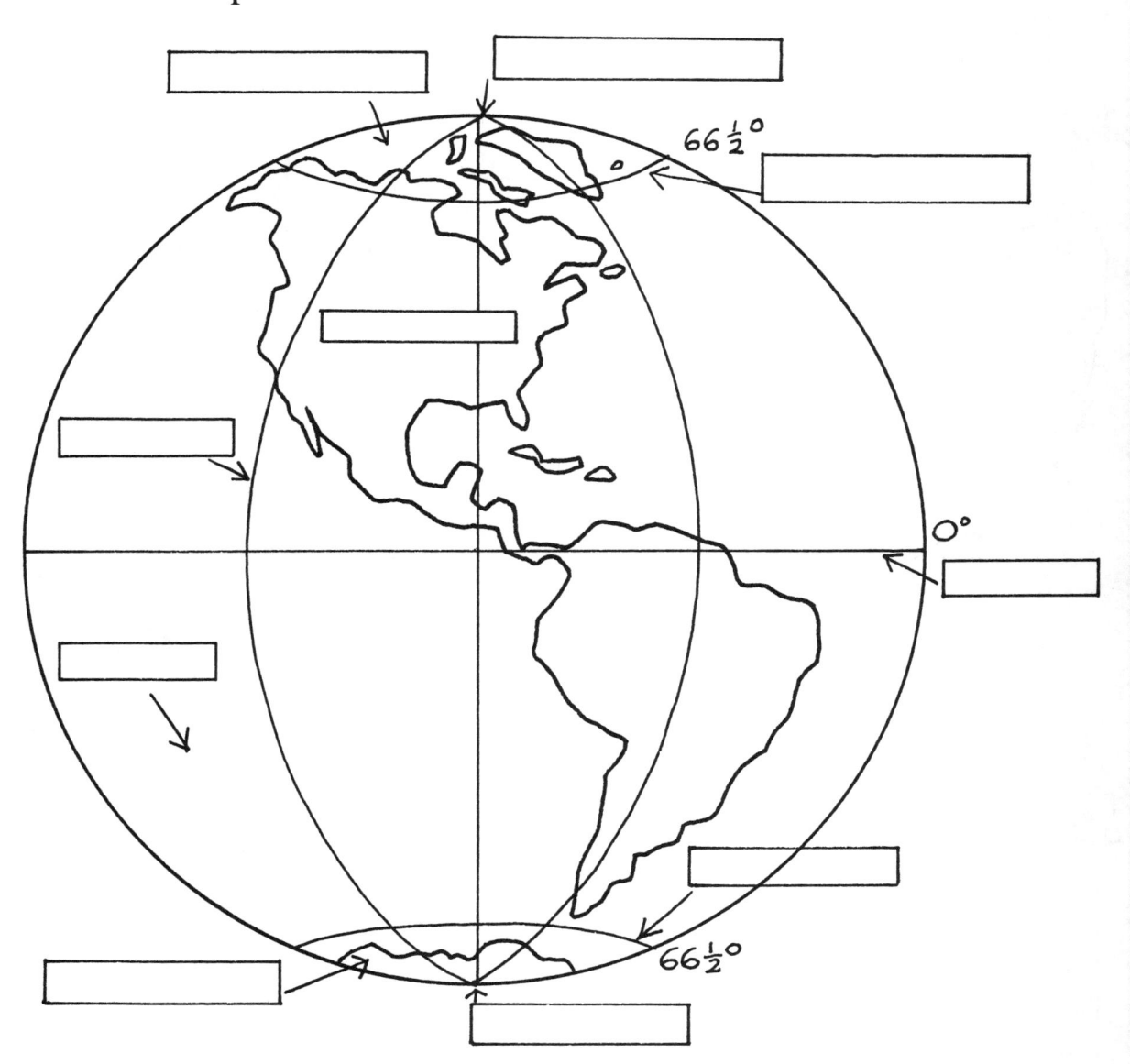

$66\frac{1}{2}°$

$0°$

$66\frac{1}{2}°$

continent	ocean	north latitude line	Arctic	North Pole
longitude line	equator	south latitude line	Antarctica	South Pole

© 1996 Troll Creative Teacher Ideas

Air Distance

Name _____

Find the approximate air distances between the cities listed below. Then fill in the grid with the distances.

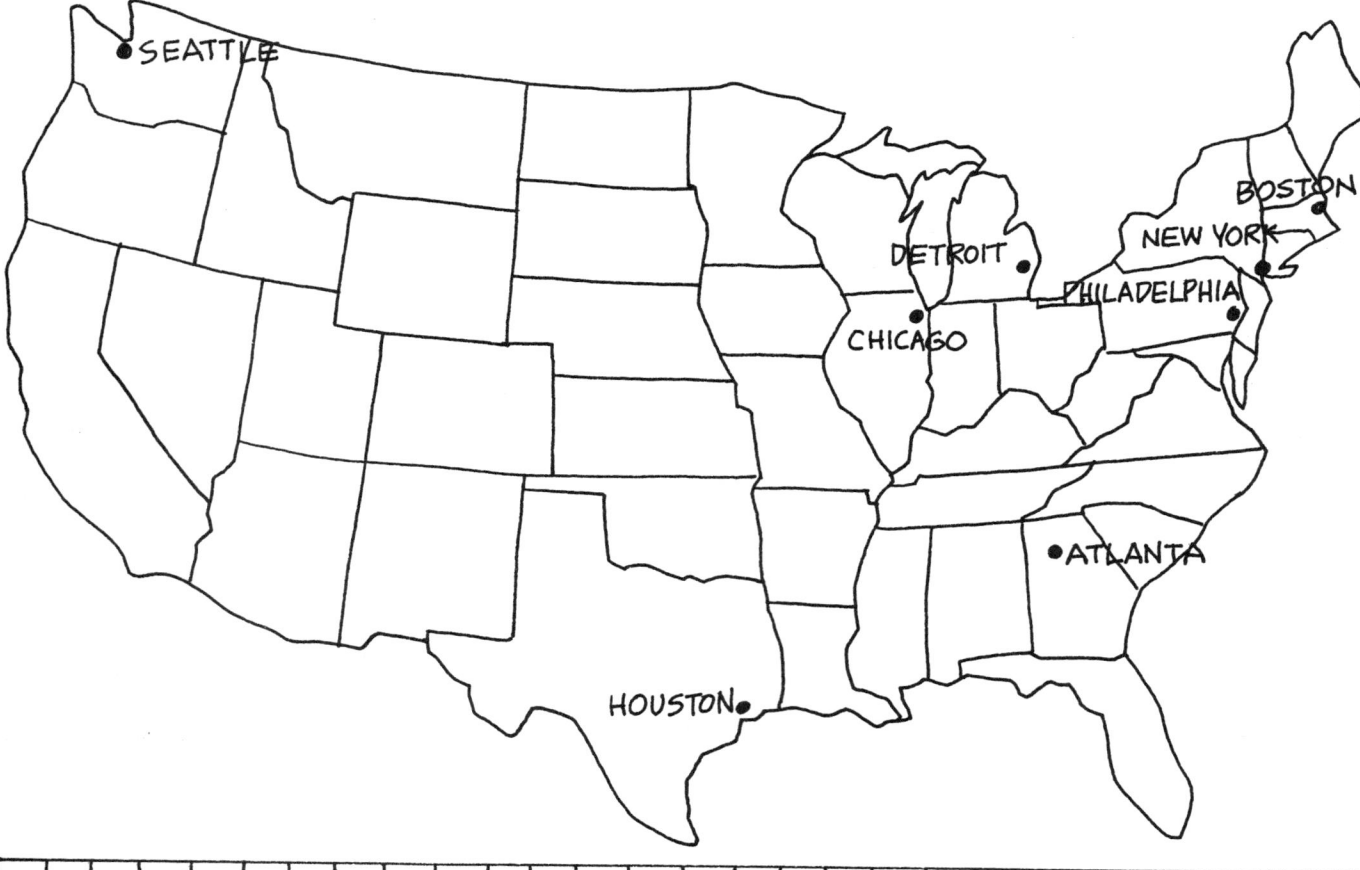

	Chicago	New York	Houston	Atlanta
Boston				
Seattle				
Detroit				
Philadelphia				

© 1996 Troll Creative Teacher Ideas

Cities and Towns

Name _____

Circle the names of the cities and towns listed below in the word search puzzle. Then try to name the state in which these cities and towns can be found.

```
R C A A N L I N D Y S E K L S H I P W
I T R L A S V E G A S W A L A S V E R
O S M A B D L A S C R R U T O N S L O
G L N S P U D E N B R I A Z T A C E R
R I O V O O Q A G O G A L L U P V B F
A L T E R L A U C S O U O U L O O S P
N V G K T D P N E T R U N L A R G E Y
D E N A H A S E T R R G A O N T Y C T
E R I T O B E R Z N Q A P L I A L L I
S O M L L S A C A R L U S D C L A V C
H H R A O L L I L A N R E B R E N S R
I C A R S R I O R A N C H O V S A L E
P N F T A A I M R A F A R M I T O N V
W P O R T C O R R A L E S F I F T Y L
R A W U A R R G R A N A T S M I L L I
E R O T M U I M G R L O S A L A M O S
C O B H S H I P R O C K O C C K Y D O
K I A E S N A L O T N E Y N R M S I L
U R U M G A L L A L B E K U R U E R A
P R S T N A R G S G A L P U P E C N M
T R U T H O R C O N S E Q U E N C E S
H N N S H E A C O R A L E F A T N A S
```

Albuquerque	Espanola	Las Vegas	Shiprock	Aztec	Farmington
Los Alamos	Silver City	Bernalillo	Gallup	Portales	Truth or Consequences
Carlsbad	Grants	Rio Rancho	Corrales	Las Cruces	Santa Fe

Graphing Temperature

Name _____

Read the chart below. Then graph the information on the line graph. Use a different-colored pen or pencil for each city. Answer the questions below the line graph.

MONTHLY NORMAL TEMPERATURE (based on records from 1951–1980)

	Jan	Feb	Mar	Apr	May	Jun	Jul	Aug	Sep	Oct	Nov	Dec
Baltimore, MD	33	35	43	54	63	72	77	76	69	57	46	37
Minneapolis, MN	11	18	29	46	59	68	73	71	61	50	33	19
Dallas–Ft. Worth, TX	44	49	56	66	74	82	86	86	79	68	56	48
San Diego, CA	57	58	59	61	63	66	70	72	71	68	62	57
Nome, AK	9	3	7	18	36	45	51	50	42	28	16	4

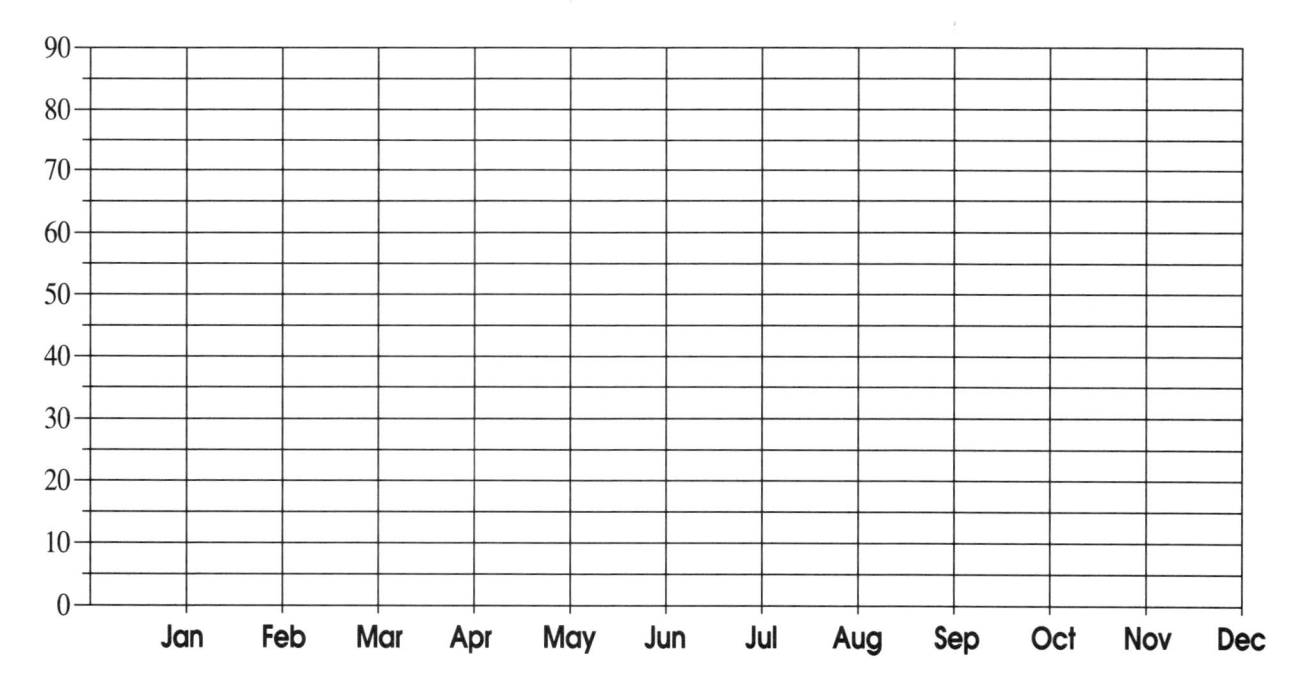

1. Which city's temperature never varies more than 15 degrees? _____
2. Which city has the highest summer temperature average? The lowest? _____
3. Which city has the coldest winters? _____
4. Name the coldest and warmest months for each city. _____

© 1996 Troll Creative Teacher Ideas

Time Line

Name _____

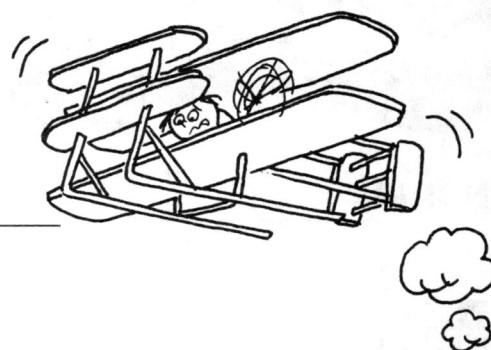

On the line provided, write the year in which each of the historical events below occurred. On a separate piece of paper, make a time line of these events. Use a history book or an encyclopedia if you need help!

1. The first successful powered airplane is launched at Kitty Hawk, North Carolina, by the Wright Brothers. _____

2. A mysterious explosion in the Tunguska region of Siberia flattens a huge area and knocks down a million trees. No meteor fragments were found and no cause has ever been determined, though many scientists believe that an icy chunk of a comet or a meteorite exploded. _____

3. Robert Edwin Peary, an American explorer, reaches the North Pole. _____

4. Roald Amundsen, a Norwegian explorer, reaches the South Pole. _____

5. The Titanic, a British passenger liner that was supposedly unsinkable, hits an iceberg and sinks, killing about 1,500 people. _____

6. The Trans-Siberian Railroad, the world's longest railroad, is completed. _____

7. Sir Edmund Hillary and Tenzing Norgay reach the summit of Mount Everest. _____

8. The Aswan High Dam on the Nile is completed, forming Lake Nasser and causing ecological changes. _____

9. The first "Earth Day" is celebrated in order to increase awareness about the environment. _____

10. In the Afar region of Ethiopia, a team led by Donald Johanson and Maurice Taieb discover the skeletal remains of "Lucy," an early human that is more than 3 million years old. _____

11. The first hole in the ozone layer of Earth's atmosphere is discovered over Antarctica. _____

© 1996 Troll Creative Teacher Ideas

Surface and Population

Name _____

Based on the information below, fill in the correct percentages in the pie graphs on page 29. Then answer the questions based on the information given in the graphs.

Continent Surfaces
Asia contains 30% of the world's land area
Africa contains 21% of the world's land area
North America contains 16% of the world's land area
South America contains 12% of the world's land area
Antarctica contains 9% of the world's land area
Europe contains 7% of the world's land area
Australia contains 5% of the world's land area

Continent Populations
Asia contains 50% of the world's population
Africa contains 11% of the world's population
North America contains 8% of the world's population
South America contains 6% of the world's population
Antarctica contains 0% of the world's population
Europe contains 24% of the world's population
Australia contains .3% of the world's population

1. Which continent has the most surface and the biggest population? _____
2. Which two combined continent surfaces equal Asia's surface area? _____
   _____
3. How much bigger is Europe's population than Australia's? _____
4. Why isn't Antarctica's population on the graph? _____
5. By the year 2025, Africa's population is expected to be greater than the populations of Europe, North America, and South America combined. What percentage of the world's population lives on these continents? If Africa now has about 11% of the world's population, estimate what its population will be in 2025. _____

© 1996 Troll Creative Teacher Ideas

Surface and Population

Name _____

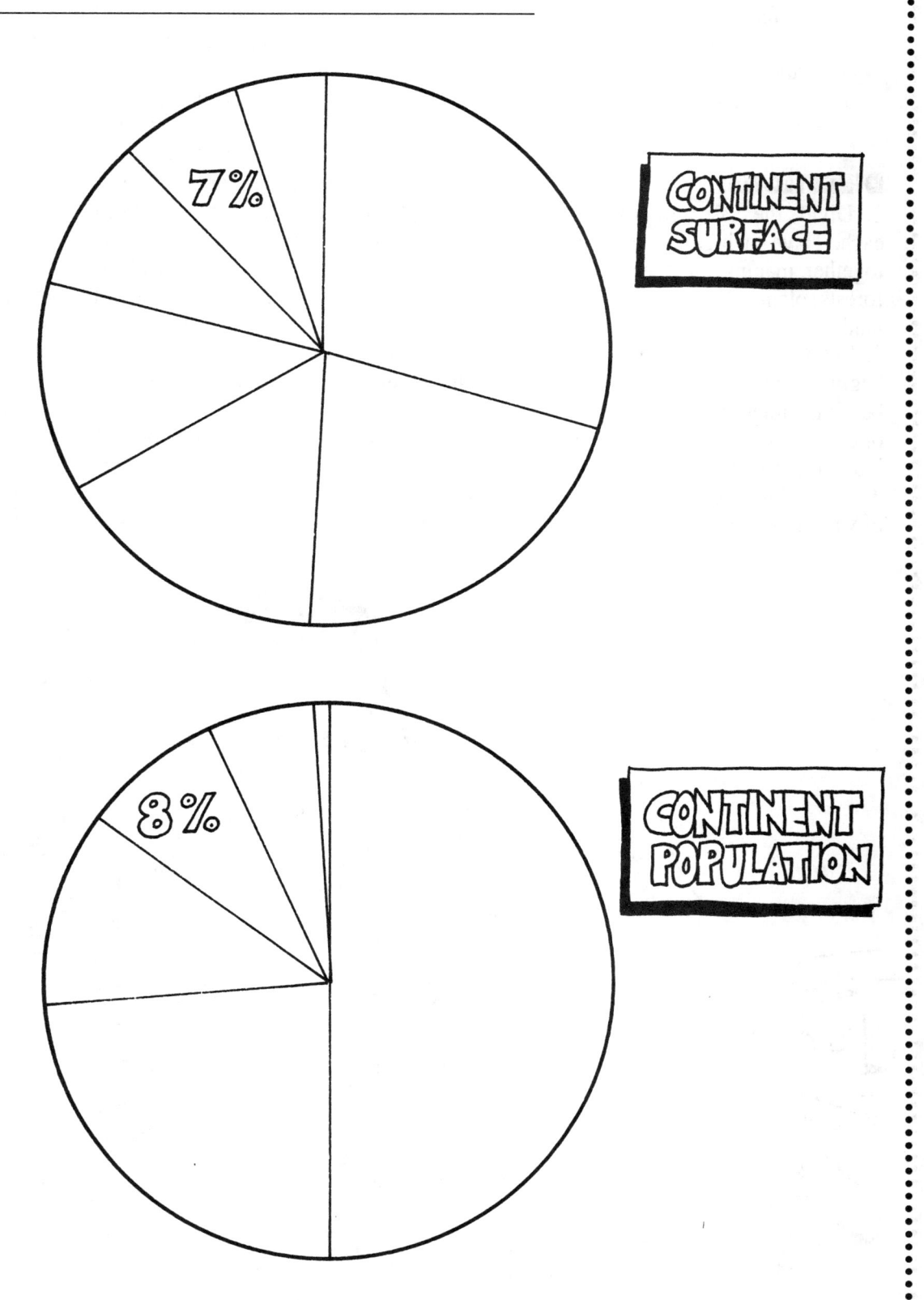

7%

CONTINENT SURFACE

8%

CONTINENT POPULATION

© 1996 Troll Creative Teacher Ideas

Model Elevations

MATERIALS:
- different-colored clays
- cardboard base, about 25" x 25"
- ruler
- craft sticks
- markers

DIRECTIONS:

1. Divide the class into groups of four or five students each. Have each group gather different-colored clays together, making sure there are colors for water, forests, plains, deserts, snow lines on mountains, and land.
2. Tell the groups to plan models showing elevation, beginning by deciding where the water and land will be. Encourage students to try to incorporate a beach or other coastline, perhaps even a peninsula or islands, into their models.
3. As the land side of the model progresses, add lots of variation in the landscaping itself as well as in altitude. For example, mountains should tower above a valley; lakes and land can be below, at, or above sea level. Students may wish to make a part near the water lush and other parts into deserts.
4. Tell each group to decide what sea level is going to be and how they will measure the altitude of the model. Use a scale for the model so that 0" equals sea level, 1" equals 1,000 feet, and so on. Using a ruler, have each group measure how high the various formations and bodies of water are from the base of the model, which is sea level.
5. When the altitude of the land and water structures have been measured according to scale, write the altitude on a craft stick and push it into the dough at the place of measurement.
6. Have students compare and contrast the altitudes on the various models. Discuss the differences in living at sea level or at high altitudes. Discover what animals and plants survive, how people adapt, and what the weather is like at the different elevations.

© 1996 Troll Creative Teacher Ideas

Race Against Time

MATERIALS:
9" paper plates
large, flat map of the world
markers
oaktag
scissors
brass fasteners

DIRECTIONS:
1. Have each student write the numbers 1 to 12 around the edges of a paper plate to resemble a clock face.
2. Make hands for the clocks by cutting oaktag scraps into short and long arrows. Position the ends of the hands in the middle of the clock face.
3. Punch a hole through the two hands and the middle of the clock face. Then attach all three together using a brass fastener. Mount each clock on a 12" x 18" piece of oaktag.
4. Tape a large, flat map of the world on a classroom wall. Create international time zones on the map. Use an encyclopedia for reference. Begin by placing the prime meridian on the map. Explain to students that the prime meridian is the zero (0°) meridian used to determine east and west longitude.
5. Place the clock posters showing the time difference in each zone as students move from the prime meridian.
6. Ask volunteers to come up and set a clock according to a given time. For example, you might say, "If the time in London, England, is 3:00, what time is it in Sydney, Australia?" Ask students to share how they came up with their answers (they must tell whether they were going from west to east or east or west) with the rest of the class.
7. During the day, ask students to tell what time it is in different cities, both domestic and foreign. Students would then consult the map to find out which cities were located in which time zones.

© 1996 Troll Creative Teacher Ideas

Map Outlines

MATERIALS:
different-colored markers
pocket folders
5" x 7" index cards

DIRECTIONS:
1. Borrow books from the library with maps of various continents, countries, and states. The maps should show both outlines and interior geographical features.
2. Draw the outline of a continent, country, or state on the cover of a pocket folder. Continue for as many areas as the class will be studying.
3. Write the name of one of the features of the place on the front of a folder in the upper left of a 5" x 7" index card. Then ask students to help think of information about the place, such as the names of forests, mountain ranges, lakes, and rivers. Write one piece of information on each card.
4. Put all the cards of each category in the appropriate folder. Go through the cards once with the class and then leave the folders on a bookshelf or in a learning center to be used during free time. Encourage students to make new cards to add to each folder. As children become more familiar with each place, see if anyone can identify the various places from their outlines on the front of the folders.

AMAZON RIVER
The longest river in South America.

BRAZIL
The South American country with the largest land mass.

© 1996 Troll Creative Teacher Ideas

Geography Picture File

Collect pictures showing land, water, sky, outer space, people, animals, plants, and other geographical subjects. These pictures may be cut from magazines, calendars, cards, travel posters, brochures, and old textbooks.

Mount the pictures on colored oaktag and laminate so the pictures in the file will stay clean and whole through the year.

Divide the class into groups of three students each. Give each group a picture from the file. Ask the groups to think about the impressions their picture gave them and write down how the picture makes them feel and any other comments they may have. Each group member may have more than one comment.

Ask each member of the group to contribute. For example, have one student be the recorder, one the fact-checker, and the third the researcher.

After the impressions and comments have been written down, each group should choose four opinions that they think are the most illustrative of their picture. Then ask each group to write the four opinions as captions for their picture.

One student in each group should then read the four captions without showing the picture. When the captions have been read, the reader may show the picture. Poll the other groups to see what impressions they formed before and after seeing the picture. Then repeat with the other groups.

Pictures may be selected from the file to hang around the room if they are relevant to a subject being studied, or they can be placed in a pocket folder to be looked at during free time.

© 1996 Troll Creative Teacher Ideas

Lost City of Atlantis

MATERIALS:
- shoe boxes or small cartons
- crayons or markers
- different types of paper
- oaktag
- scissors
- modeling clay or dough
- thread
- yarn
- collage materials
- glue
- tape
- brass fasteners

DIRECTIONS:
1. Tell the the class about the myth of Atlantis. People have claimed there once was a city called Atlantis that was swallowed by the ocean. Some people believe that Atlantis survived underwater and still exists. Scientists believe that the mythical Atlantis was an island called Santorini, or Thera, in the Aegean Sea. Data indicate that the volcano Santorini erupted in approximately 1500 B.C. and destroyed the island.
2. Ask the class for comments about the probability of a volcano erupting and causing the ocean to swallow an island. Do they think an island could survive under the water? Could people adapt to underwater life so suddenly? Would their personal effects as well as their buildings and plant life be able to withstand the environmental change? Brainstorm about how the people of Atlantis might have survived the eruption and what their life is like under the sea.
3. Borrow books from the library to research this time period and what life was like in the region of the Aegean Sea. Encourage students to discover how the people dressed, what their governments were like, what their cities looked like.

4. Ask each student to make a diorama showing how Atlantis might look. Have students bring in shoe boxes or cartons for their dioramas, and provide them with oaktag, modeling clay or dough, and various collage materials. Encourage children to think about the way Santorini might have looked back in 1500 B.C. when creating their dioramas.
5. Make an Atlantis gallery. Set the dioramas on tables or desks around the room and invite the class to browse through them. Allow plenty of time for observations and discussions.

© 1996 Troll Creative Teacher Ideas

Games from Afar

To play a cooperative learning game from Israel, instruct each student to bring in a hat from home. Divide the class into groups of six. Give each group a rope long enough for everyone to hold with two hands.

Create a home base for each team. Next, gather the hats from each group and place them in piles about 20 feet from their home bases.

Groups begin the game standing on their home base. At a signal, each member of each group grabs the rope with two hands. The team then runs to its own pile of hats. The object of the game is to put on the hats without using hands. Team members may help each other by using their knees, feet, teeth, elbows, or in whatever way they can imagine. If any member of a team lets go of the rope, that team is disqualified. The first group to get their hats on and run back to their home base is the winner.

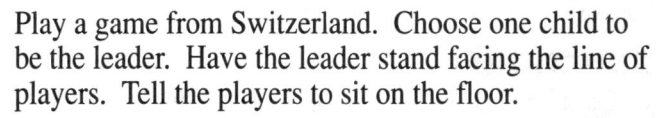

Play a game from Switzerland. Choose one child to be the leader. Have the leader stand facing the line of players. Tell the players to sit on the floor.

Give the leader a small ball or a beanbag. To play, the leader tosses the ball or beanbag to someone and calls out at the same time, "Name the animal. The first letter is *T*."

The player to whom the ball was tossed then catches it and asks, "Is it a turkey (or other "t" name)?" If "turkey" is correct, that player becomes the new leader and the old one goes to stand in the line of players. If the answer is incorrect, the leader throws the ball to the next player and asks the same question. Whoever answers correctly becomes the new leader.

If the leader goes through the whole line with no correct answers, he or she starts the next round with, "Name an animal. The first two letters are *TU*."

For added challenge, let the leader toss the ball to anyone in line instead of in line order. He or she should still make sure all players get a turn.

Geographical Interactive Poster

MATERIALS:
- large piece of oaktag
- 3" x 5" index cards
- crayons or markers
- construction paper
- Velcro
- plastic storage bag
- glue

DIRECTIONS:

1. On a large piece of oaktag, draw an outline of the town, city, state, or country where the class lives, or of an area the class is studying. Decide what aspect of the chosen location should be the focus of your poster, such as products manufactured, natural resources, land or water features, climate, landmarks, or historic sites. For example, if Washington state were chosen, you might focus on trees as an important natural resource. (Washington state is used as an example below.)

2. After drawing an outline of Washington in the center of the sheet of oaktag, ask students to research varieties of trees that grow in Washington. Draw these forests in appropriate places within the outline.

3. Brainstorm with the class about wood products. Ask students to draw pictures of the products on index cards (for example, chairs, homes, baseball bats, and paper), and of nonwood items as well.

4. Attach a small piece of the soft side of Velcro to the backs of these pictures. Place small pieces of the hard side of Velcro in and around the outline of the state.

5. Place the index cards in a large plastic storage bag and hang it next to the poster on a wall or a bulletin board. Students can stick the pictures that show wood products onto the poster, leaving those items that are not made of wood in the storage bag.

6. You may also wish to use this type of poster to help students learn the names of the countries in each continent. Begin by drawing an outline of a continent and the boundaries between countries. Leave out the names of each country, but place a small piece of the hard side of Velcro within each border.

7. Write the names of the continent's countries on index cards and attach bits of the soft sides of Velcro to the backs. Students can then place the names of countries in their proper places on the map. For added challenge, make name cards for countries not located on the featured continent as well.

8. Other game subjects include the states and their capitals, and natural resources and their locations within a particular geographic area.

© 1996 Troll Creative Teacher Ideas

Geography Bulletin Board

MATERIALS:
- blue bulletin-board paper
- stapler
- large sheets of white paper
- tape
- crayons or markers
- scissors
- Velcro
- 3" x 5" index cards
- hole puncher
- yarn
- glue

DIRECTIONS:
1. Staple blue bulletin-board paper to the board.
2. Have students tape large sheets of white paper together to form one larger sheet. On this paper, draw the outline of the area to be studied. Cut around the edges.
3. On the outline, draw in any land and water features located in the area. Add other information, such as elevation markings, boundary lines, animals and plants living there, roads, railroads, and airports. Color the map.
4. Attach pieces of Velcro (hard part) to the features in the map. Staple the map onto the center of the bulletin board.
5. On index cards, write the geographic terms for various features in the area, such as: peninsula, mountain range, lake, island, waterfall, volcano, airport, and feet above or below sea level.
6. Punch a hole in the center of the top of each index card. Then tie one end of a 24" length of yarn to each card. Staple the cards around the map on the bulletin board.
7. On the free end of the yarn lengths, wrap a piece of Velcro (soft part). Title the board, "Do You Know Your Geography?"
8. To use the board, students will match up names of features with the symbols for those features on the map. Have students attach the yarn from the index cards to the Velcro located on the matching feature.

© 1996 Troll Creative Teacher Ideas

States Word Search

Name _____

Find the names of all 50 states hidden in the word search puzzle below. The words may be written forward, backward, up, down, or diagonally.

```
O L O C A L I F O R N I A I N I G R I V W O
M I S S O U R I A T O K A D H T U O S E H N
A A I I W L H D N A L S I E D O H R T A A O
W N N E V A D A R N E E R A W A L E D I N R
I A W A I V E R M O N T A D D A N I A R I T
S I C O T O A K A N S A S I A L A S K A L H
C S O D Y N G E O D G I K R O Y W E N L O D
O I N L K N O G E R O H I O V W I I D A R A
N U N O C N E M V A D Z A L I Y L I I B A K
S O E N U G A Y O N O R E F R O L A N A C O
I L C A T O S E N N I M O N R M I W D M H T
N O T G N I H S A W I O W A G I N A I A T A
P C I I E K A R T S E T C E I N O H A T U I
O A C H K N S E A H E H S A N G I F N G O N
E S U C R M X J O X T S R I E M S R A E S I
E S T I P A Y W A R O E T O K L A H O M A G
S A U M S I T E O E N A R K A N S A S O K R
S M A R Y L A N D N K G O C I X E M W E N I
E H W Y I N G P E I I P P I S S I S S I M V
N M A I N E W T A A K S A R B E N E W R Y T
N C O L O R A D O M A S S A C H U S E T T S
E U S E R I H S P M A H W E N E W H A G P E
T T T E S S P E N N S Y L V A N I A N S W W
```

Alabama	Massachusetts	South Carolina	Alaska	Michigan	South Dakota
Arizona	Minnesota	Tennessee	Arkansas	Mississippi	Texas
California	Missouri	Utah	Colorado	Montana	Vermont
Connecticut	Nebraska	Virginia	Delaware	Nevada	Washington
Florida	New Hampshire	West Virginia	Georgia	New Jersey	Wisconsin
Hawaii	New Mexico	Wyoming	Idaho	New York	Illinois
North Carolina	Indiana	North Dakota	Iowa	Ohio	Kansas
Oklahoma	Kentucky	Oregon	Louisiana	Pennsylvania	Maine
Rhode Island	Maryland				

World Map Jigsaw Puzzle

Reproduce the map once. Color the map and mount it on oaktag. Cut the map apart along the dotted lines. Then ask students to put together the puzzle pieces to form a world map. Store the puzzle pieces in an envelope.

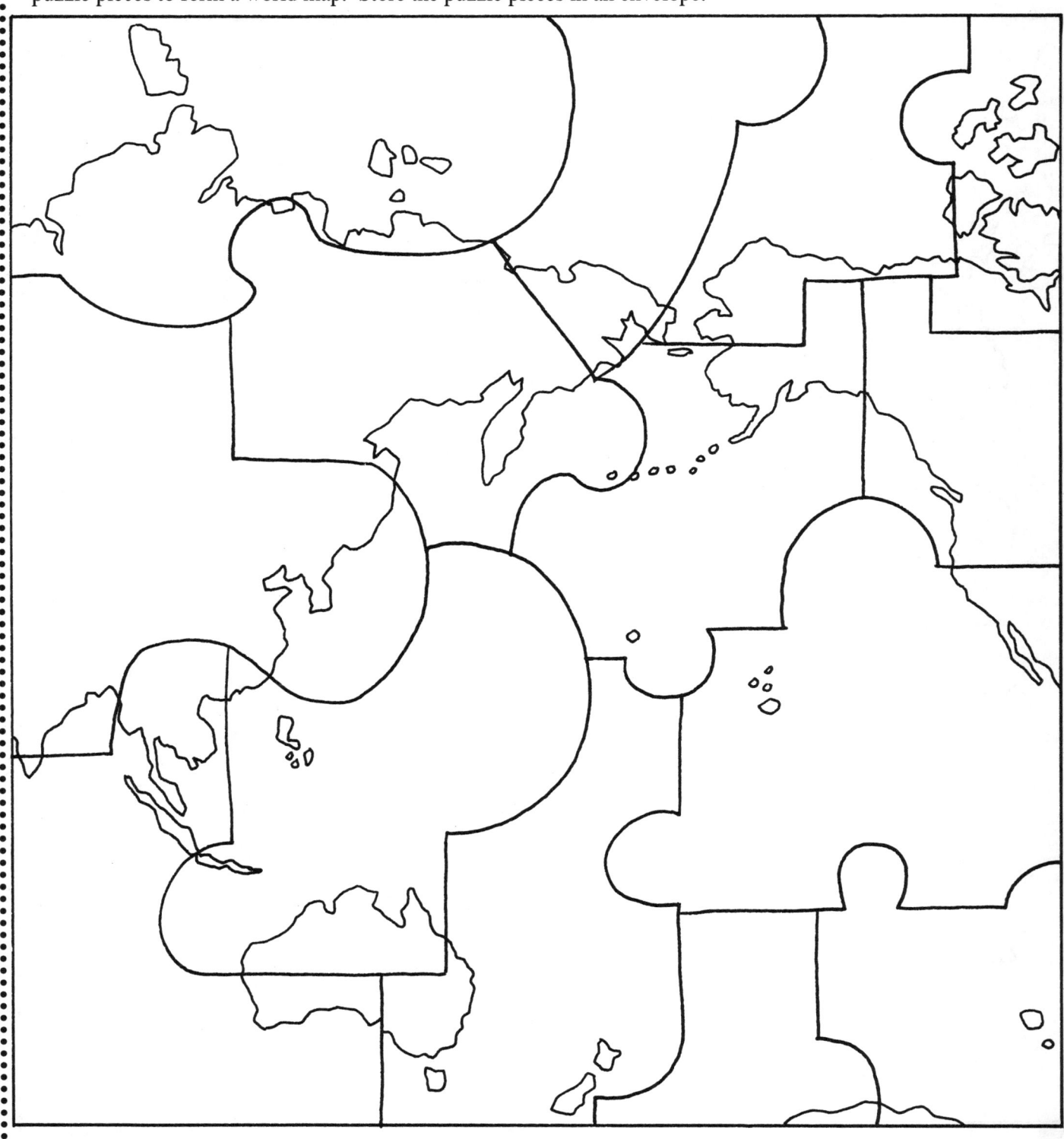

© 1996 Troll Creative Teacher Ideas

World Map Jigsaw Puzzle

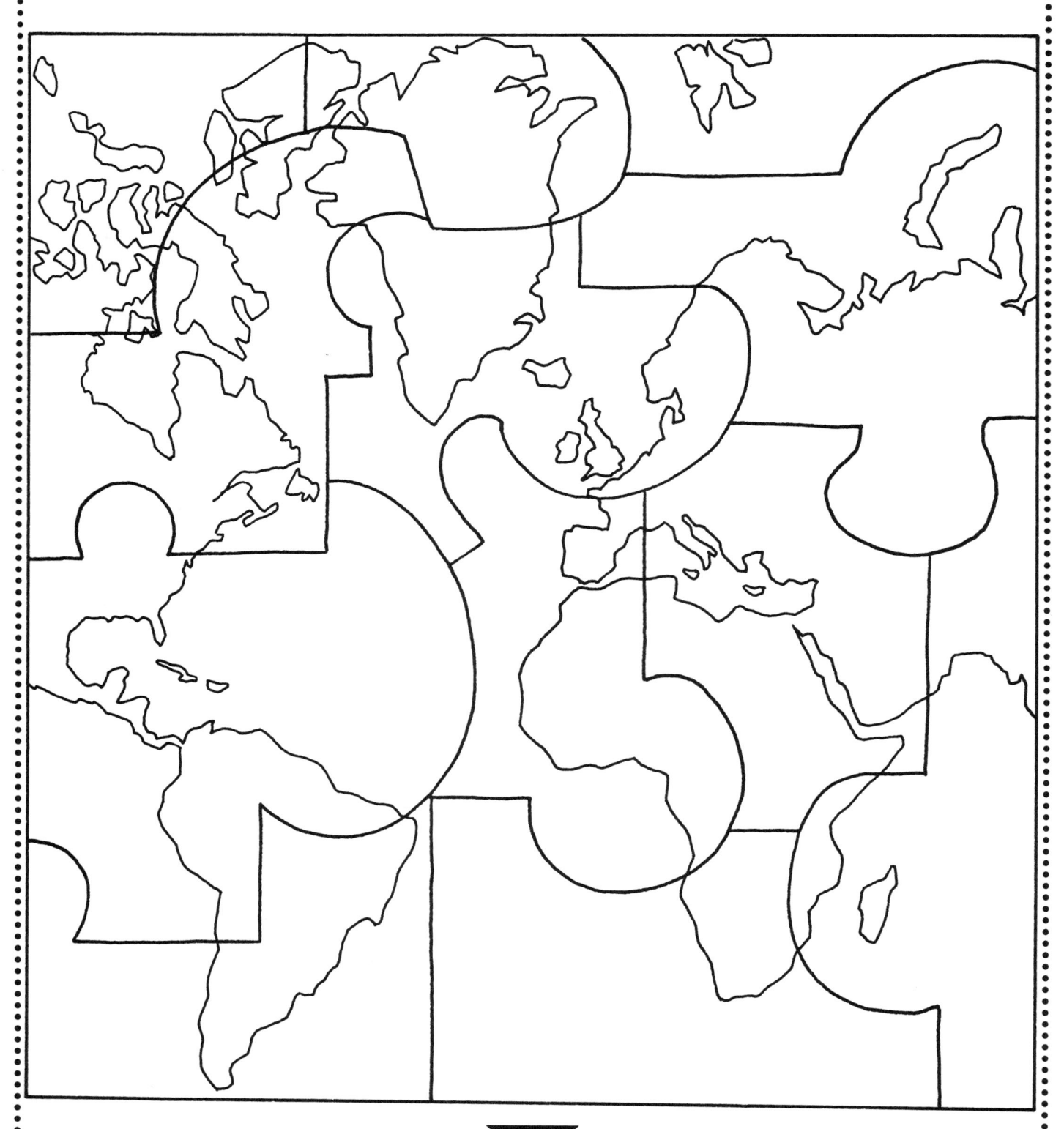

40

© 1996 Troll Creative Teacher Ideas

Sopaipillas Recipe

MATERIALS:
- 4 cups flour
- 3 teaspoons baking powder
- 1 teaspoon salt
- 3 tablespoons shortening
- water
- vegetable oil
- honey

Approximately 48 servings

DIRECTIONS:
1. Ask several children to sift together flour, baking powder, and salt.
2. Use two knives or a pastry blender to add in shortening.
3. Have a small group of students add 3 tablespoons of water at a time, mixing it with the dry ingredients. The dough should be of medium-thick consistency.
4. Help several students roll out the dough to about 1/4" thick. Then cut the dough into 3" squares or other shapes.
5. Pour oil into a pot and heat it. Gently drop the sopaipillas into the oil, a few at a time. Fry them until golden brown. Serve plain or with honey.

© 1996 Troll Creative Teacher Ideas

Fiesta Eggs

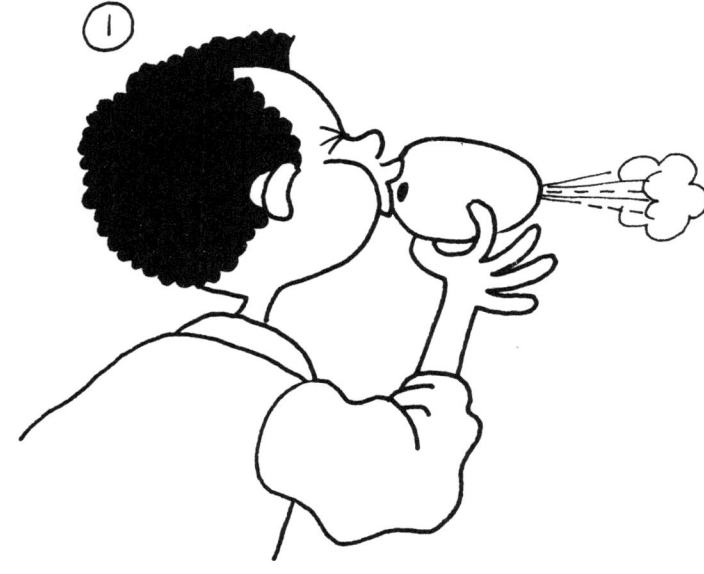

MATERIALS:
- raw eggs
- blunt needles
- different-colored construction paper
- scissors
- pipe cleaners
- tape
- paint and paintbrushes

DIRECTIONS:
1. Poke a hole at either end of a raw egg, then gently blow the inside out.
2. Enlarge one hole once all the yoke is out.
3. Cut confetti from different-colored construction paper. Gently put the confetti inside the eggs.
4. Tie a knot on one end of a pipe cleaner. Insert the knotted end into the larger hole in the egg.
5. Tape the pipe cleaner in place, as shown. Then tape the egg closed.
6. Paint the outside of the eggs very gently. Hang the eggs to dry from a clothesline.
7. During a celebration, or to mark the beginning or end of a holiday or party, students may break their eggs and watch the confetti fly.

Descriptive Words

Name _____

Read the place name in each box, and then write down three adjectives to describe it. Use reference books if you are not familiar with a name. Then discuss your responses with a classmate.

Alaska	Puerto Rico	Australia
_____	_____	_____
_____	_____	_____
_____	_____	_____

England	Siberia	Switzerland
_____	_____	_____
_____	_____	_____
_____	_____	_____

Germany	Sahara Desert	South Africa
_____	_____	_____
_____	_____	_____
_____	_____	_____

Kenya	Egypt	China
_____	_____	_____
_____	_____	_____
_____	_____	_____

© 1996 Troll Creative Teacher Ideas

Through the Rain Forest

Name _____

It's a jungle out there! Try to find your way from Start to Finish in this rain forest maze.

© 1996 Troll Creative Teacher Ideas

Abbreviated States

Name _____

Write the full name of each of the following states on the blank line next to its abbreviation. Use reference books or a telephone or postal directory if you are not familiar with an abbreviation.

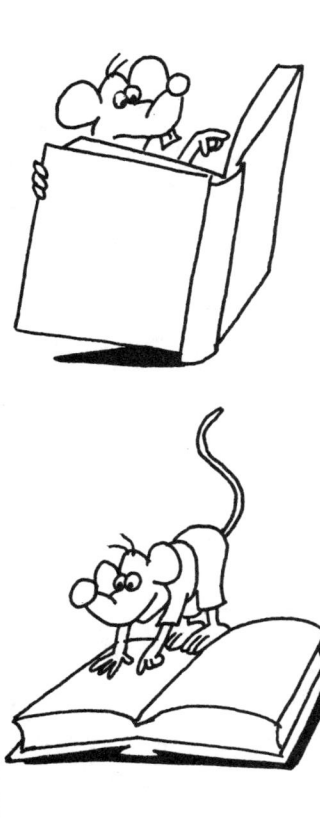

AZ _____
CO _____
DE _____
IN _____
KY _____
LA _____ 
MD _____
NV _____
OK _____
PA _____ 
RI _____
SD _____
TX _____
UT _____
VA _____
WY _____

© 1996 Troll Creative Teacher Ideas

Places Puzzles

Name _____

Write the name of a continent, country, state, city, landmark, or other geographical term that begins and ends with the letters given.

Example:
D __alla__ s
A __fric__ a
S __heffiel__ d

S _____ a   D _____ m
E _____ e   A _____ a
A _____ s   M _____ d

P _____ s   D _____ e
A _____ s   I _____ k
S _____ a   K _____ i
S _____ p   E _____ d

G _____ f   M _____ a
U _____ l   E _____ s
L _____ u   S _____ e
F _____ g   A _____ m

T _____ n   R _____ d
O _____ w   O _____ a
W _____ o   A _____ o
N _____ t   D _____ r

© 1996 Troll Creative Teacher Ideas

Statistics Pie

Name _____

Use the statistics in the chart below to complete the information in the pie graph. (Hint: Round off figures to the nearest ones place. Together, they equal 100%.)

Population Growth (based on U.S. Census 1980–1990)

	POPULATION	AREA (in square miles)	POPULATION GROWTH
Albuquerque, NM	384,736	95	15.6%
Anchorage, AK	226,338	1,732	29.8%
Boston, MA	574,283	46	2%
Colorado Springs, CO	281,140	103	30.7%
Little Rock, AR	175,795	79	10.5%
Oklahoma City, OK	444,719	604	10.1%

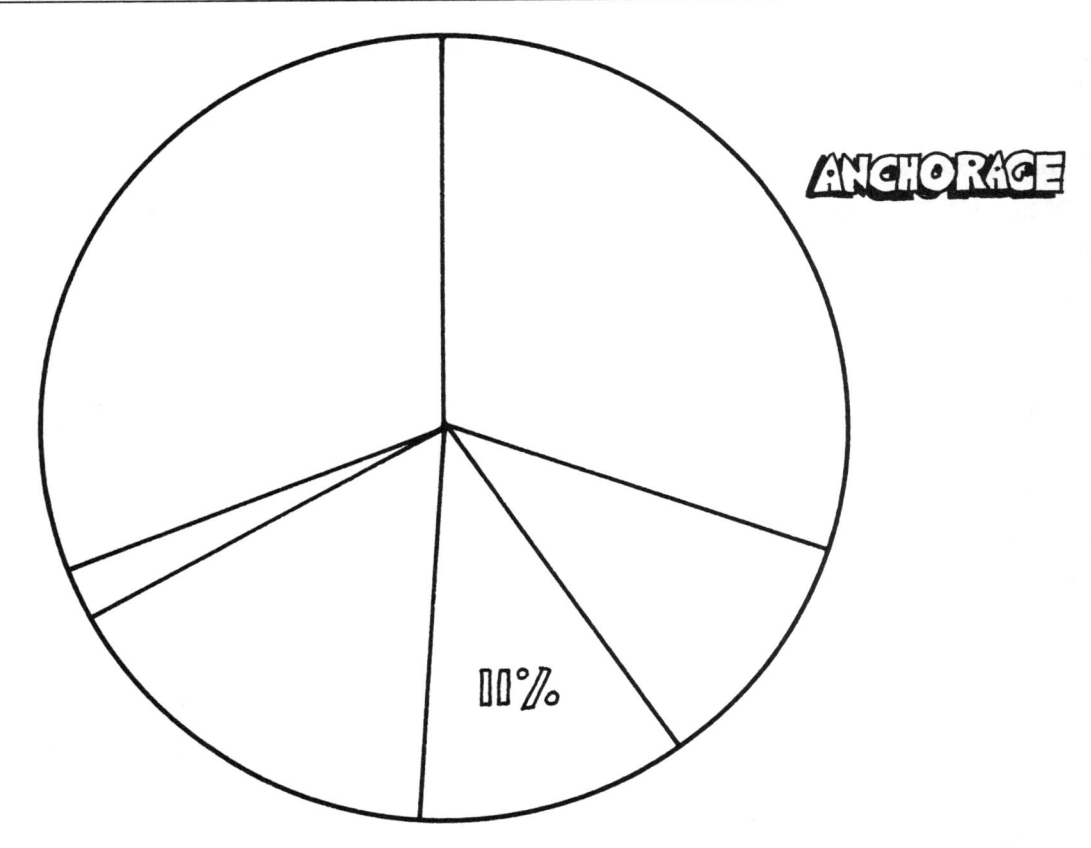

ANCHORAGE

10%

BONUS: On a separate piece of paper, list some reasons why a city might gain or lose population over the course of ten years.

© 1996 Troll Creative Teacher Ideas

What's Wrong Here?

Name _____

Read the short paragraphs below. Then find the sentence or sentences in each that does not make sense. Rewrite the sentences on the lines provided at the end of each paragraph.

1. Volcanoes and earthquakes occur because parts of our planet are always moving. The earth's crust is divided into huge sections called plates. When the plates move—against each other, away from each other, or directly head-on—the hot magma under the crust is able to seep out of the cracks made by the moving plates. Once out of the earth, the magma quickly turns to water and cools the land upon which it falls, slowing the process of eruption.

_____

_____

2. Dolphins are mammals whose home is the sea. They like warm waters and can be found along at least one coast of every continent. Dolphins live in families or larger groups, each led by the male with the most strength. When dolphins sleep, they float in the water with their heads below the surface and tails hanging down. With a small movement of their tail, they rise to the surface to breathe about every thirty seconds, without ever waking up. Dolphins are carnivores, although they have no teeth. As a result, most are now switching over to a diet of seaweed and other ocean plants.

_____

3. Lightning can be extremely dangerous. It is capable of causing fires in homes and forests. It can damage power lines and cause major black-outs. There are different types of lightning: within a cloud, from cloud to cloud, between cloud and air, and from cloud to ground. Lightning is rarely accompanied by thunder. Since sound travels faster than light, a way to tell how close a storm is to you is to count the seconds between the sound of thunder and the lightning flash.

4. Hawaii became the 50th state of the United States on August 21, 1959. Located to the Northwest of the United States, part of it borders on one of Canada's territories, the Yukon. Hawaii's islands were all created by repeated volcanic eruptions. Pineapple is the chief product of Hawaii.

_____

_____

© 1996 Troll Creative Teacher Ideas

Worldwide Words

Name _____

The words in the box below are from many different languages around the world. Read each word carefully. Then write each word under the correct heading.

hogan	flat	escargot
tortilla	palazzo	kimono
kilt	turban	villa
plantains	brogans	veil
sushi	sari	hut
mango	pueblo	drindl
poi	yurt	sarong

Eat it?   Live in it?   Wear it?

© 1996 Troll Creative Teacher Ideas

Finding the Similarities

Give each student a 3" x 5" index card. Ask each child to write his or her full name in the center.

In the upper right corner, ask the class to write three words they would use to describe themselves. In the lower right corner, ask them to write three activities they like to do.

In the upper left corner, ask the class to write where they and their parents were born. In the lower left corner, have them write what they would like to be when they are adults.

After everyone has finished their cards, encourage the class to walk around the room reading other students' cards. Instruct each student to find at least two classmates with something similar to his or her own biography.

When the class is seated again, ask questions to see what they have discovered about each other. Some suggested questions:

> Did you find someone who has a similar ethnic background?
> Is there anyone who described themselves as friendly? Cranky?
> Did anyone have similar hobbies or favorite sports?
> Who was born the farthest away?
> Whose parents were born in another country?
> Who would like to be a writer when he or she becomes an adult? A doctor? A teacher?

Match Idioms

Name _____

All languages have colorful phrases called idioms. An idiom is an expression of speech whose meaning must be taken figuratively instead of literally. For example, "He's full of hot air" does not mean that a person really is filled with hot air; it refers to a person who talks on and on.

Read the idioms in each column below. Then draw lines to match the idioms in the first column to those in the second column that have similar meanings.

1. Don't bite off more than you can chew.
2. To eat crow.
3. Go fly a kite!
4. Let's get back to the subject.
5. You can't make a silk purse from a sow's ear.
6. Don't waste your breath!
7. Go jump in a lake!
8. Give him an inch, he'll take a mile.
9. He's as slow as molasses.
10. There's always room for one more.
11. To go out for wool and come home shorn.
12. Are you standing on one leg?

a. Where six can eat, seven can eat.
b. Don't take a step longer than your leg.
c. Give him a hand and he takes a foot.
d. Save your saliva!
e. To swallow the toad.
f. Go fry asparagus!
g. Let's get back to our sheep.
h. To have the tables turned.
i. Are you in a hurry?
j. He creeps like a bedbug.
k. A monkey dressed in silk is still a monkey.
l. Go whistle in the ocean!

Culture Crossword Puzzle

Name _____

Read the clues below about different cultures and customs. Then write the answers in the corresponding spaces.

Across
1. Ancient people who built pyramids to use as tombs.
4. Traditional Inuit shelter.
6. Form of medical treatment done by sticking thin needles in particular parts of the body.
10. Until 1990 division between East and West Germany in the city of Berlin (two words).
11. Traditional Native American home, usually made with animal skins.
12. Native American tribe of the Southwest.

Down
2. Traditional language of people living in Ireland or Scotland.
3. Water from this Egyptian river is used for cooking, cleaning, drinking, washing, and watering crops.
5. System formerly used in South Africa to separate people by race.
6. Name of the continent to which the kangaroo is native.
7. Instead of using an alphabet, Chinese writing uses these things to represent words.
8. The skirt worn by men in Scotland on special occasions.
9. Weapon used by Inuits in Greenland to hunt narwhals in summer.

© 1996 Troll Creative Teacher Ideas

World Travelers

MATERIALS:
- crayons or markers
- scissors
- glue
- large piece of oaktag
- 3" x 5" index cards
- playing pieces

DIRECTIONS:
1. Reproduce the game board on pages 54-55 once. Color the game board, cut it out, and mount the pieces together on a large piece of oaktag.
2. Reproduce the game cards on page 56 four times. Color the cards, mount them on oaktag, and cut them apart.
3. To make the question cards, write a question on an index card about a geographic area that the class is currently studying. For example, if the current unit is about South America, some questions may be:

> Where is the rain forest located?
> In what country or countries are the Andes mountains located?
> What is the main export of Brazil?
> What language is spoken in Argentina?
> What native tribe lived in Peru long ago?

4. Write the correct answer on the back of each card. Write "+1" or "+2" at the bottom of each card to indicate the number of spaces a player may move ahead if he or she answers the question correctly.
5. Use playing pieces from another game, or use a penny, nickel, dime, and quarter.

HOW TO PLAY:
(for two to four players)
1. Put the question cards in a stack next to the board. Place the special site cards aside until needed.
2. The youngest player goes first. That player draws a card from the question pile and tries to answer it. If correct, he or she may move ahead the indicated number of spaces. If the player is incorrect, the next player goes.
3. Play continues around the board, with each player trying to answer a question. Players may move in either direction. When a player lands on a special site, he or she may collect that card.
4. The first player to collect all six of the special site cards is the winner.

World Travelers

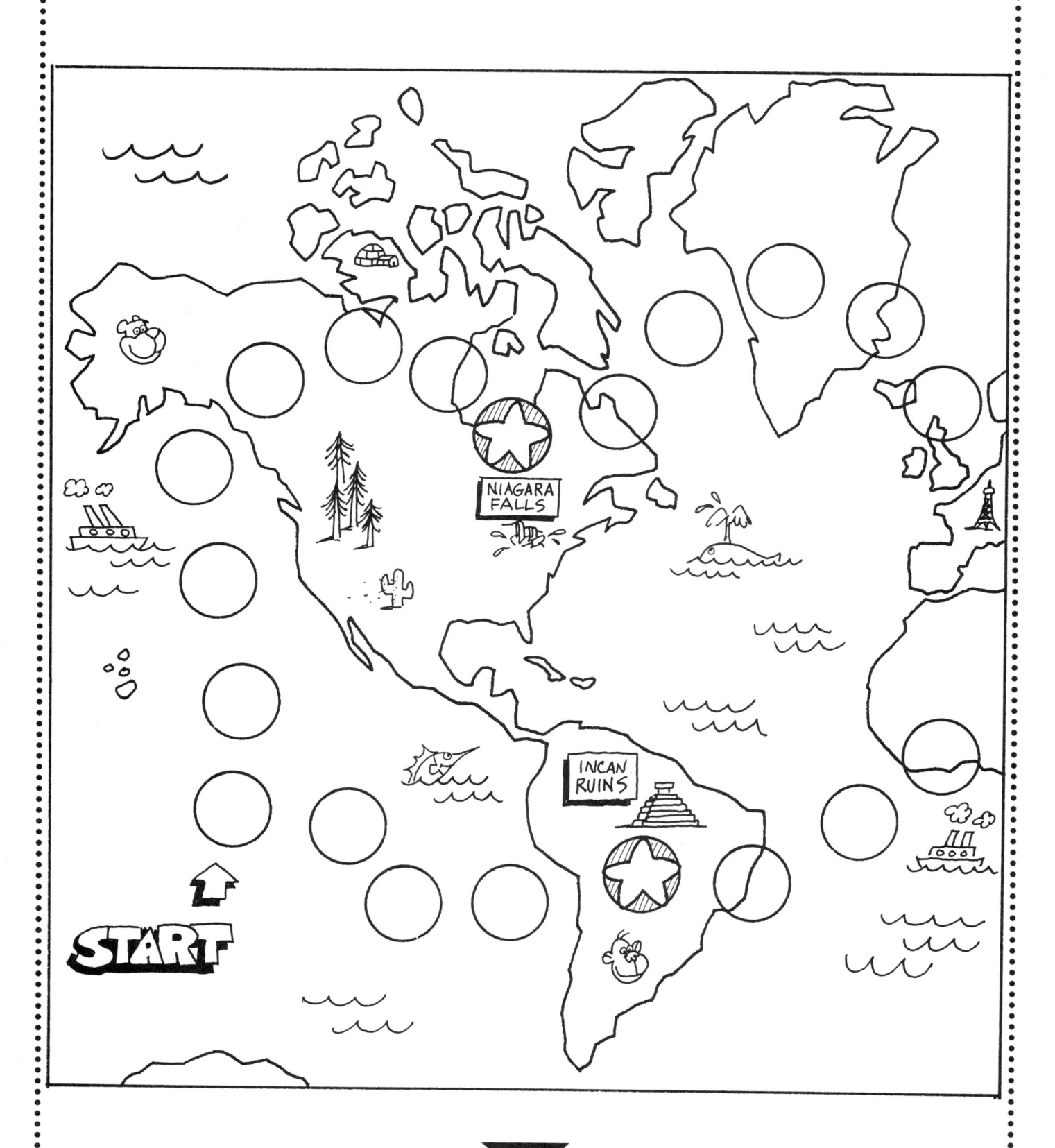

NIAGARA FALLS

INCAN RUINS

START

54

© 1996 Troll Creative Teacher Ideas

World Travelers

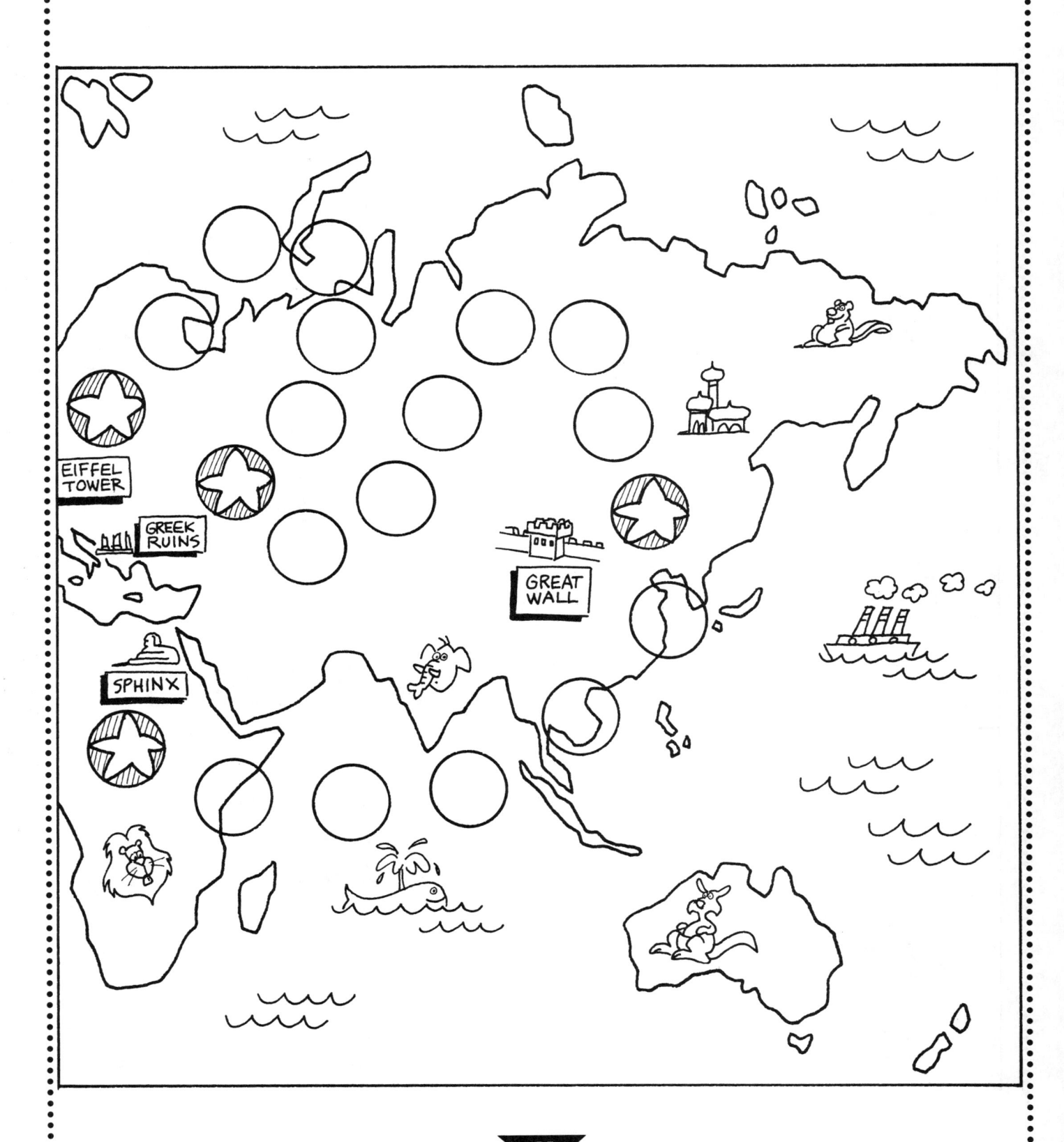

EIFFEL TOWER

GREEK RUINS

GREAT WALL

SPHINX

55
© 1996 Troll Creative Teacher Ideas

World Travelers

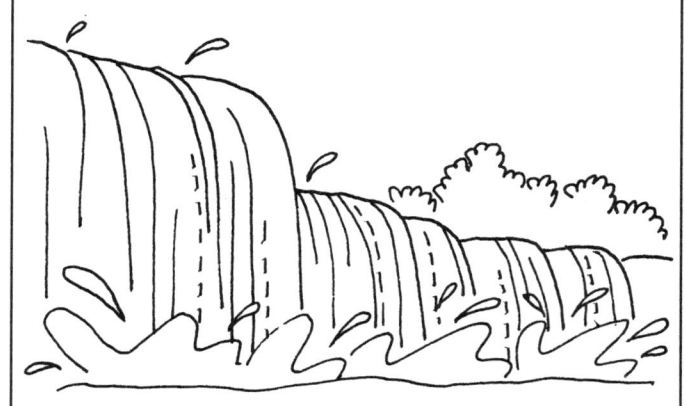

INCAN RUINS

NIAGARA FALLS

SPHINX

EIFFEL TOWER

GRECIAN RUINS

GREAT WALL OF CHINA

Where in the World Is It?

Name _____

Use a map of the world with latitude and longitude lines to answer the questions below.

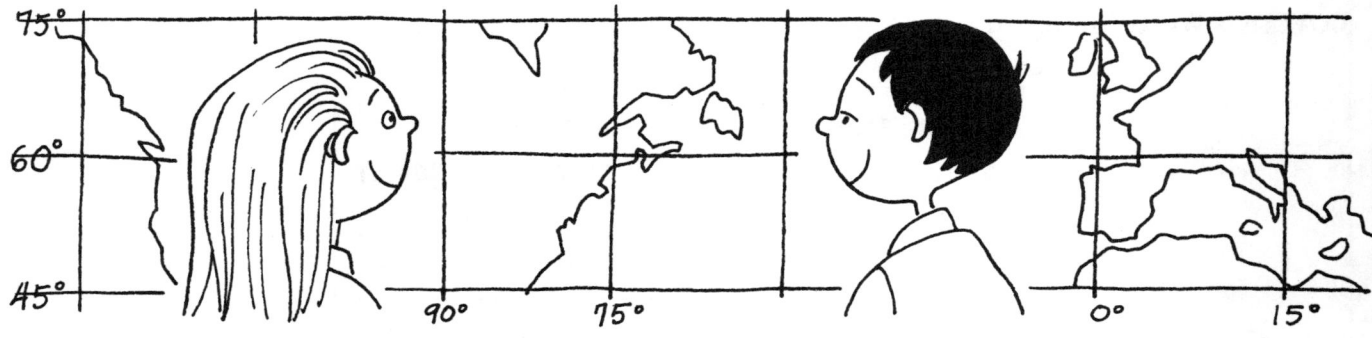

1. Which U.S. state is located at 40 degrees North latitude and 120 degrees West longitude? _____

2. Which capital is located nearest 10 degrees South latitude and 80 degrees West longitude? _____

3. In South America, what mountain range runs from 10 degrees South latitude to 75 degrees South latitude? _____

4. What capital is located nearest 60 degrees North latitude and 10 degrees East longitude? _____

5. What sea can be found at 30 degrees East longitude between 50 degrees North and 40 degrees North latitude? _____

6. What small country lies between 120 degrees East and 130 degrees East longitude and directly on the Tropic of Cancer? _____

7. What lake lies on the equator between 30 degrees East and 40 degrees East longitude? _____

8. What bay lies between 80 degrees East and 100 degrees East longitude and south of the Tropic of Cancer? _____

© 1996 Troll Creative Teacher Ideas

World-Famous Explorers

Name _____

Map an important voyage of one of the explorers below. Mark highlights of the travels with a star on the map. On the lines provided, explain what important discoveries were made on this voyage.

Leif Eriksson	Marco Polo
Vasco da Gama	Ferdinand Magellan
John Cabot	Ponce de León
Sir Francis Drake	Robert Edwin Peary

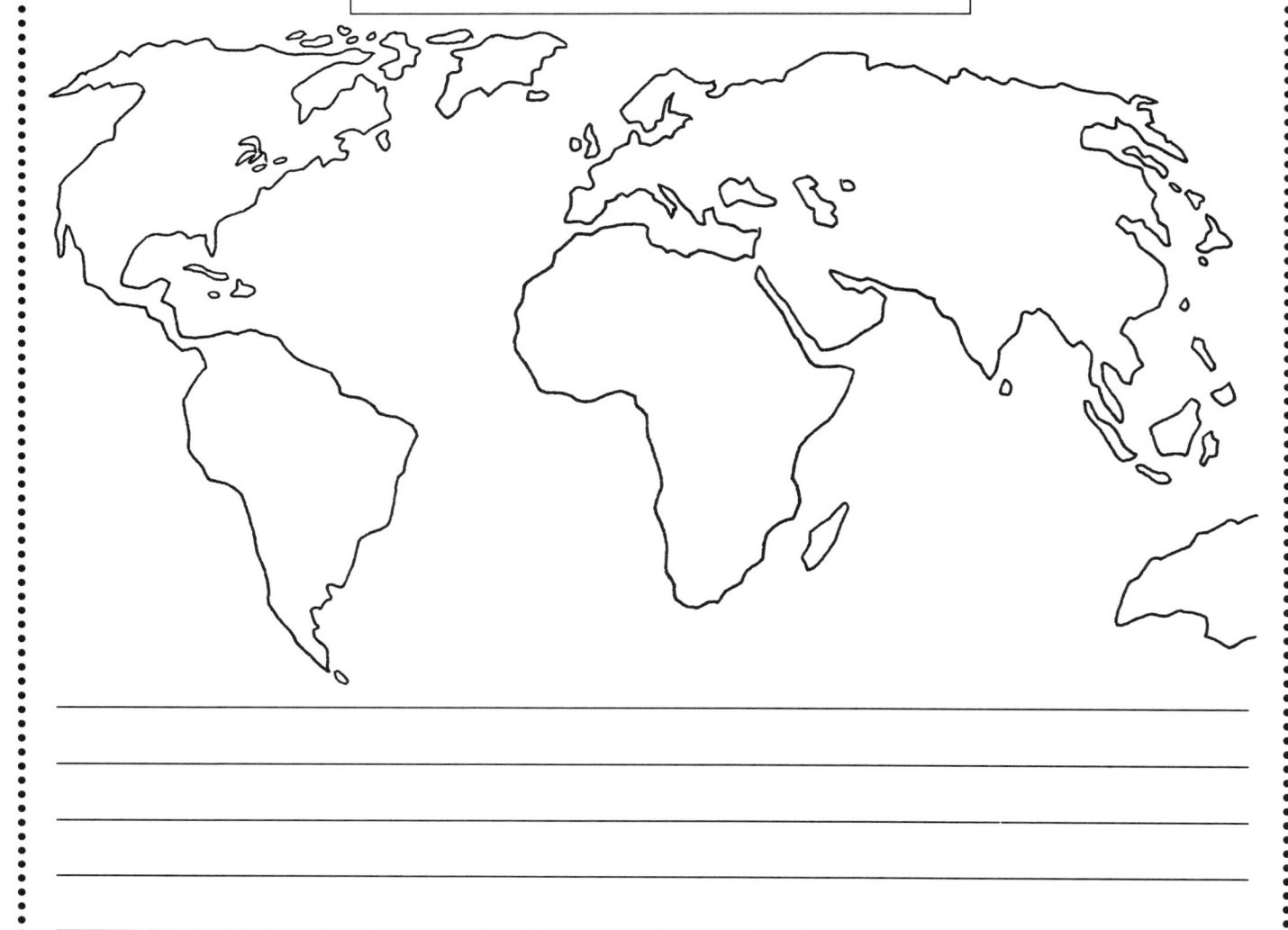

_____
_____
_____
_____

© 1996 Troll Creative Teacher Ideas

Shortest Routes

Name _____

Look at the map below. Find the shortest route from Western City to Luluville for these methods of transportation:

        sailing ship   kayak   car   walking

Use a blue pen to show the best boat route, a red pen to show the kayak route, a green pen to show the car route, and a black pen to show the best walking route.

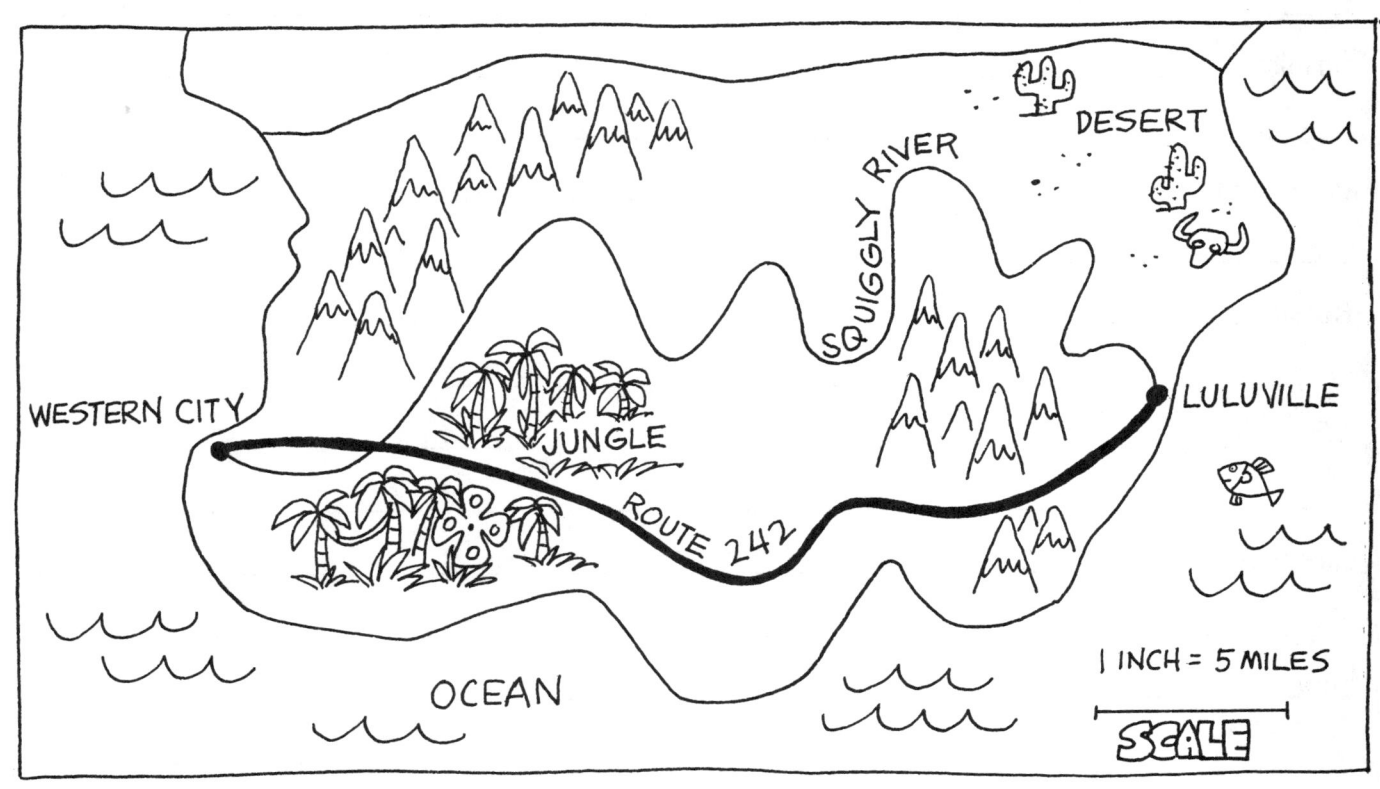

[Map showing Western City on the left connected by Route 242 to Luluville on the right, with Jungle, mountains, Squiggly River, Desert, and Ocean features. Scale: 1 INCH = 5 MILES]

Which of these methods of transportation do you think would be the fastest?
_____

What problems might you expect along the way? _____
_____
_____
_____

© 1996 Troll Creative Teacher Ideas

Worldly Chitchat

Name _____

Locate the places where each of the languages below are spoken. Write the names of the countries or regions on the lines provided. Use an encyclopedia if you need help!

English _____
_____

Spanish _____
_____

Portuguese _____
_____

Russian _____
_____

Mandarin _____
_____

Japanese _____
_____

Hindi _____
_____

Arabic _____
_____

Farsi _____
Tagalog _____
Swahili _____
Siouan _____

Ecosystems of the World

Name _____

Fill in the map of the Western Hemisphere below to indicate where the various ecosystems are found. Use the key provided below.

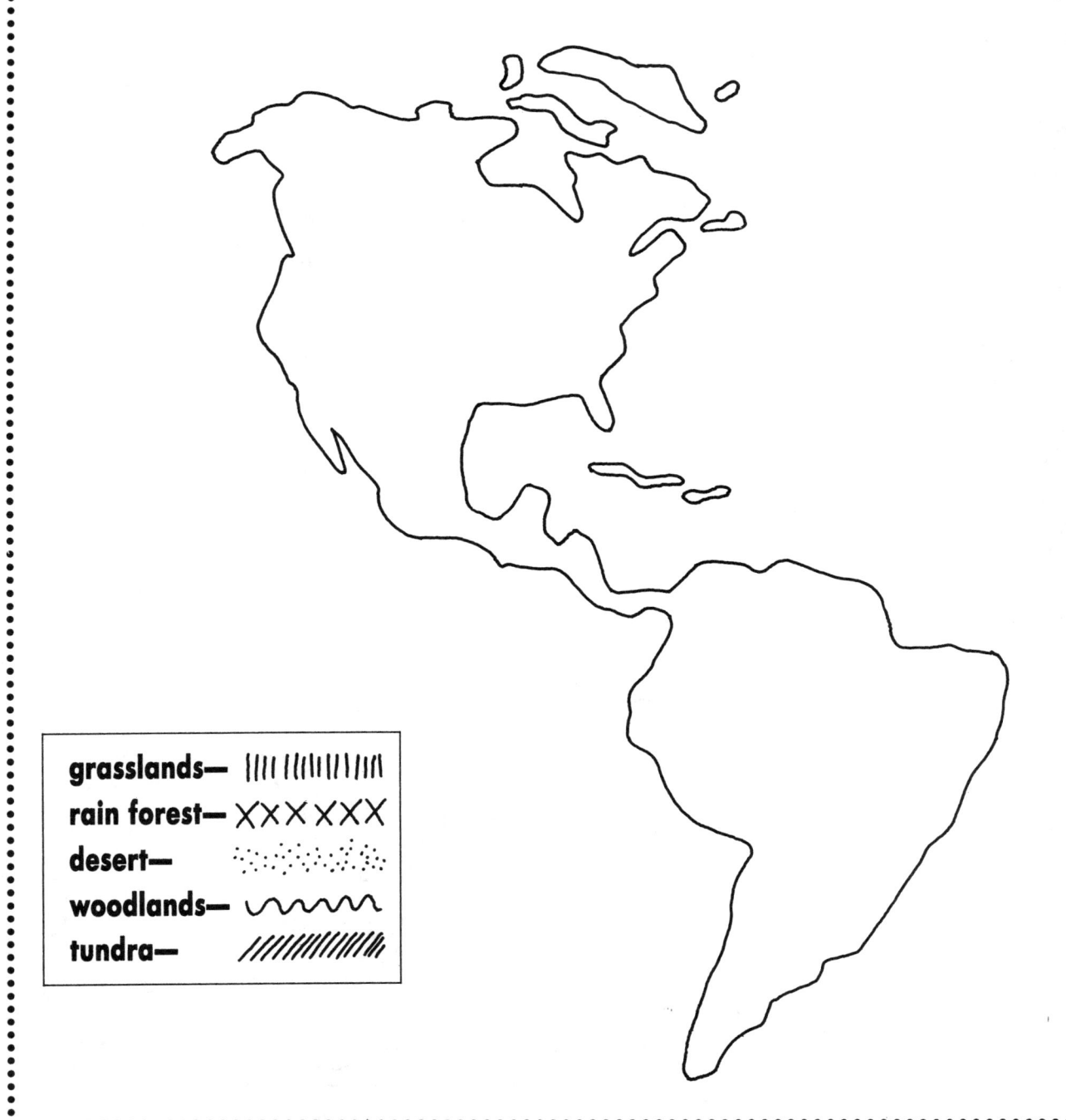

grasslands— ||||| |||||||||||||
rain forest— ××××××
desert— ∴∵∴∵∴
woodlands— ∽∽∽∽
tundra— ////////////

Ecosystems of the World

Name _____

Fill in the map of the Eastern Hemisphere below to indicate where the various ecosystems are found. Use the key provided below.

grasslands—	||||/||||||||||
rain forest—	XXXXXX
desert—	:·.·:·.·:·.·:
woodlands—	∿∿∿∿
tundra—	/////////////

© 1996 Troll Creative Teacher Ideas

Historical Clues

Name _____

Look at each of the maps of the United States below. Then write the approximate year each map represents on the line provided beneath it. If you need help, use an encyclopedia or a history book!

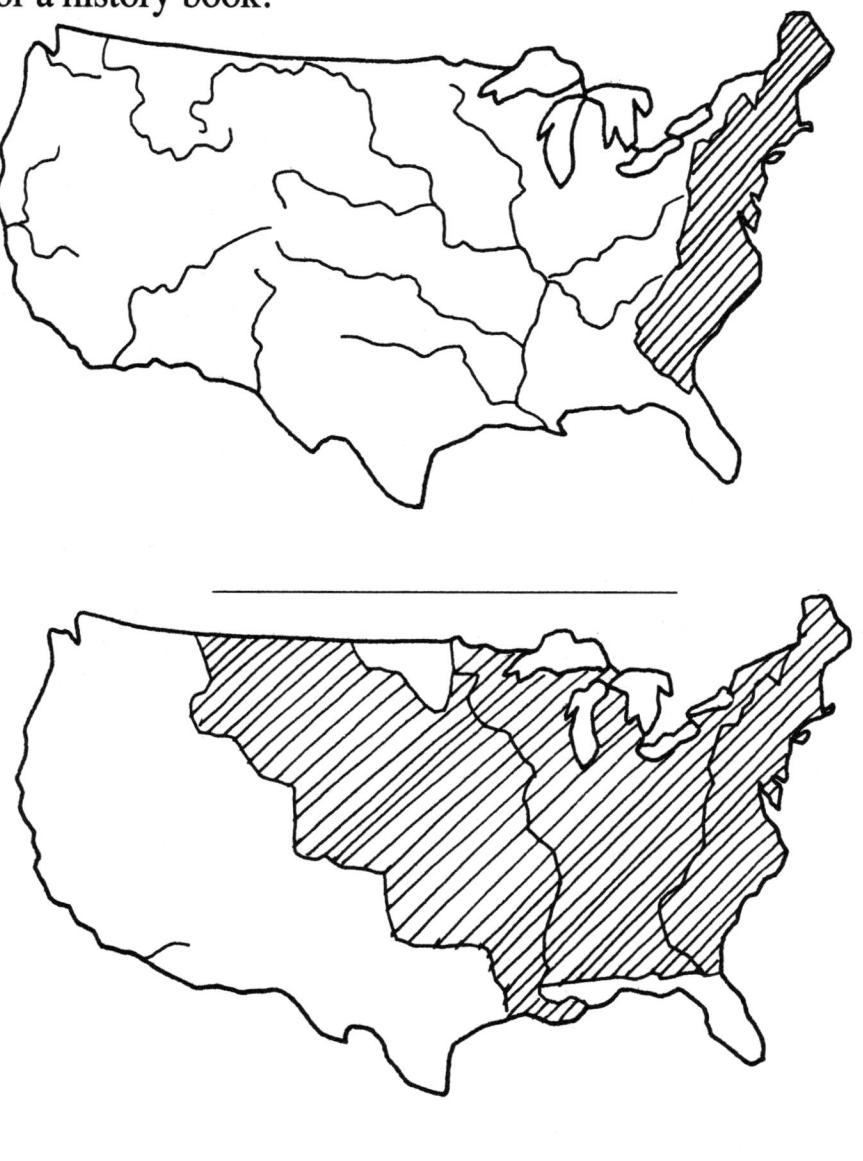

_____

_____

On a separate piece of paper, tell what important event led to the addition of the Louisiana Purchase. Then write an imaginary dialogue between two people involved in the Louisiana Purchase.

Topographical Test

Name _____

A *topographical* map shows the physical features of a particular region. Study the topographical map of Saturday Island below. Then answer the questions on the lines provided.

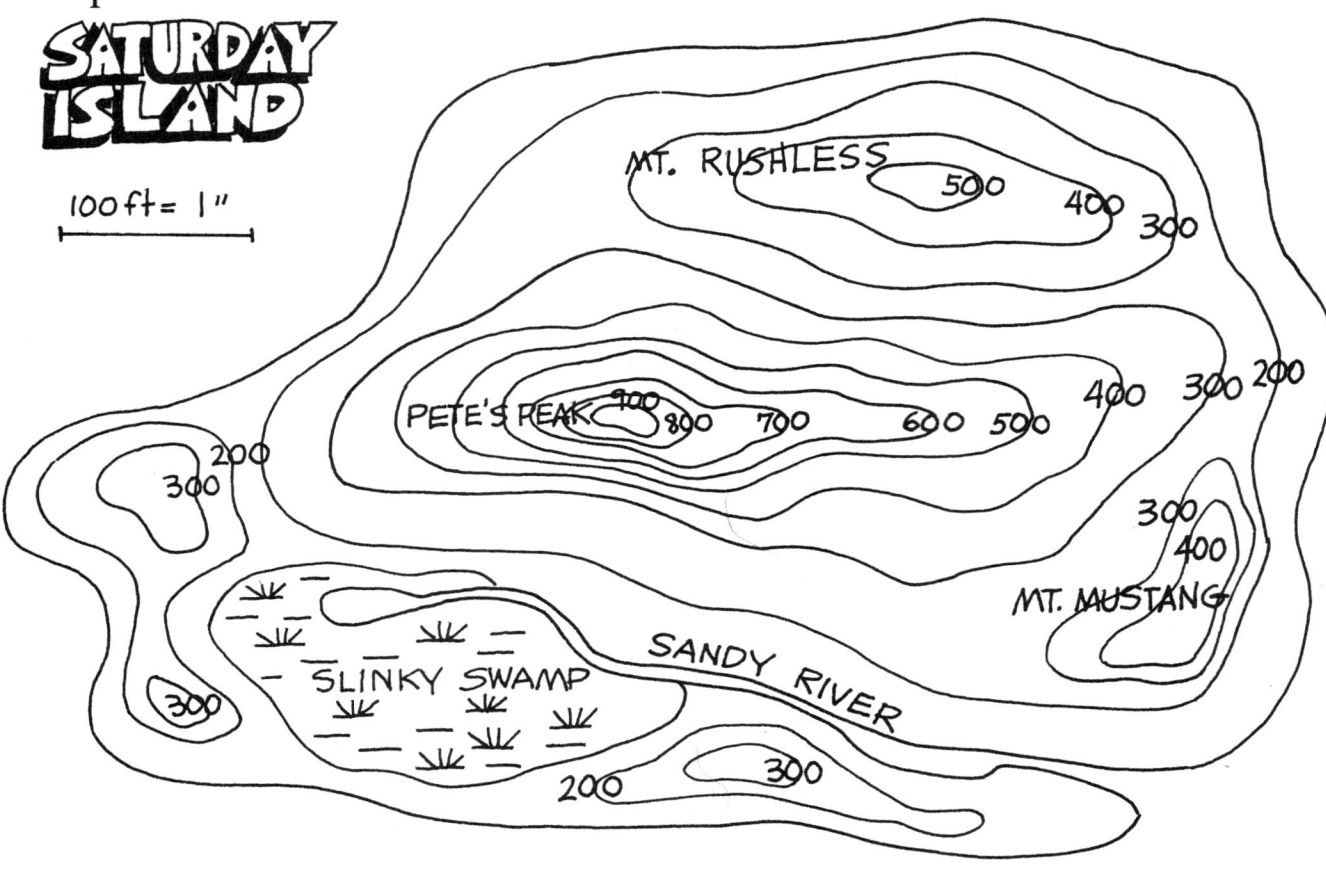

SATURDAY ISLAND

100 ft = 1"

MT. RUSHLESS 500 400 300

PETE'S PEAK 900 800 700 600 500 400 300 200

200 300

300

300 400 MT. MUSTANG

SLINKY SWAMP

SANDY RIVER

200 300

1. What is the highest elevation point on Saturday Island? _____
2. What is the approximate elevation of Slinky Swamp? _____
3. What is the elevation of the shortest peak on the island? _____
4. Which mountain has the most gradual slope? _____
5. What is the lowest elevation point on Saturday Island? _____

BONUS: Draw a topographical map of your own imaginary island!

Mountain Madness

Name _____

A *cartographer* is a person who draws and designs maps. Our cartographer has misplaced the labels for the map of world mountain ranges and systems. Write the correct letter next to each mountain range or system to help her complete the map.

- **A.** Urals
- **B.** Caucasus
- **C.** Atlas
- **D.** Brooks
- **E.** Andes
- **F.** Rockies
- **G.** Pyrenees
- **H.** Appalachian
- **I.** Alps
- **J.** Himalaya

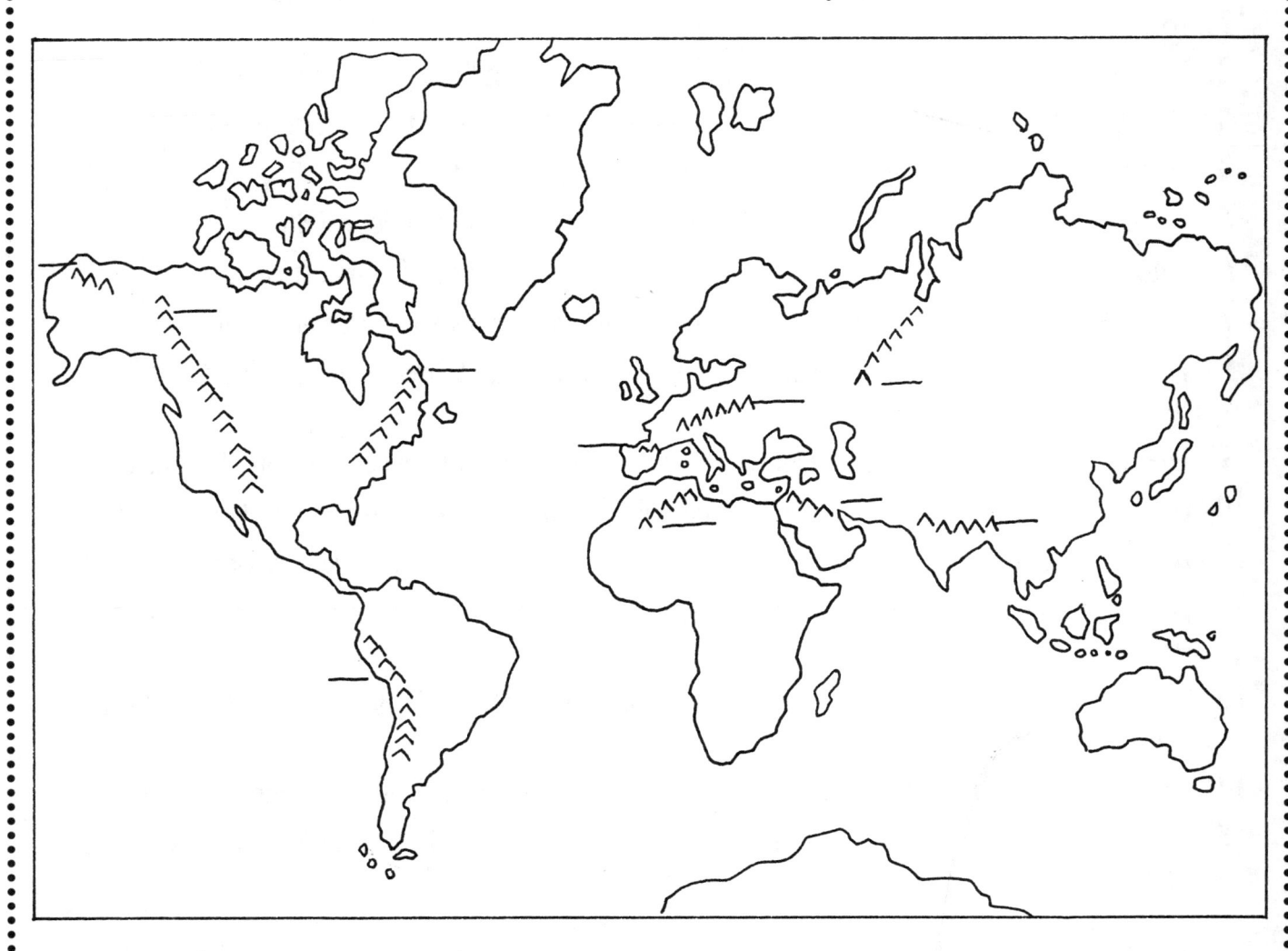

© 1996 Troll Creative Teacher Ideas

Muddled Maps

Name _____

The master map thief has struck again—and he has meddled with the Mudville map! Help Police Chief Ethel fill in the missing parts of Mudville. Then read the clue at the bottom of page 67 to find out where the map thief is hiding.

1. Town Hall is located on Acorn Street.
2. The street that runs east–west and is located north of Acorn Street is Chestnut Street.
3. The street that runs east–west and is located south of Acorn Street is Walnut Street.
4. First Street is a north–south street. It is the westernmost street in town.
5. The north–south streets are numbered in order from First Street to Fourth Street.
6. Mudville School is located on the northeast corner of Walnut and Second streets.
7. Sam's Market is located on the west side of Fourth Street between Acorn and Walnut streets.
8. The Mudville Library is located on the south side of Chestnut Street between Third and Fourth streets.
9. The Post Office is located on the north side of Chestnut Street between First and Second streets.
10. Betty's Bookstore is located on the east side of First Street between Acorn and Chestnut streets.
11. Al's Pizza is located on the west side of Second Street between Walnut and Acorn streets.
12. Dr. Dragon's office is located on the east side of Fourth Street between Acorn and Chestnut streets.
13. The Soda Shoppe is located on the south side of Chestnut Street between Second and Third streets.
14. CD Heaven is located on the south side of Walnut Street between First and Second streets.
15. The Hip Hop Clothing Shop is located on the south side of Acorn Street between Second and Third streets.

© 1996 Troll Creative Teacher Ideas

Muddled Maps

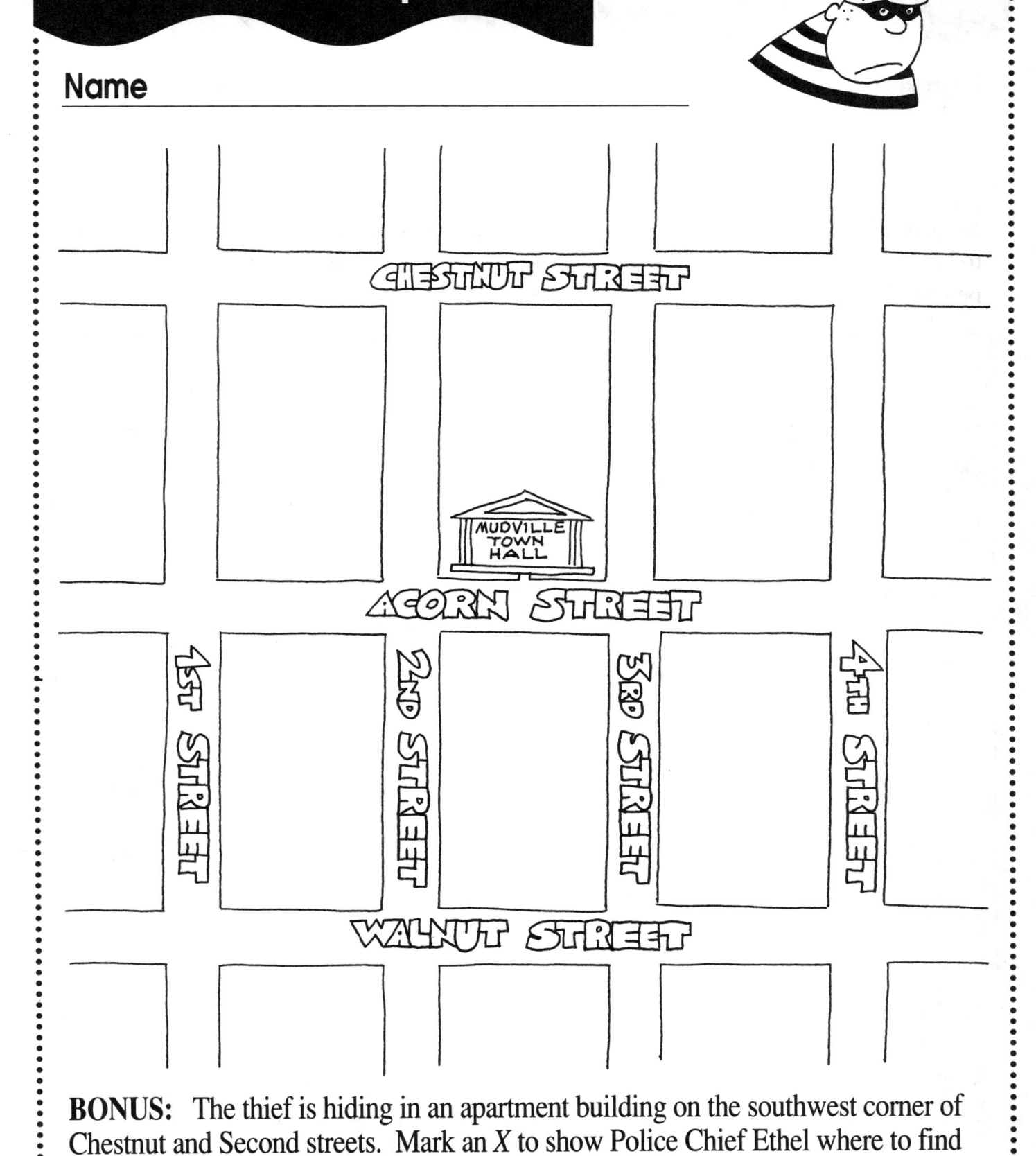

Name _____

CHESTNUT STREET

MUDVILLE TOWN HALL

ACORN STREET

1ST STREET 2ND STREET 3RD STREET 4TH STREET

WALNUT STREET

BONUS: The thief is hiding in an apartment building on the southwest corner of Chestnut and Second streets. Mark an *X* to show Police Chief Ethel where to find him!

© 1996 Troll Creative Teacher Ideas

City Slickers

Name _____

Do you know where the world's greatest cities are located? Look at the dots on the map below. Next to each dot, write the letter of the city name given in the list below. If you need help, use an atlas or encyclopedia.

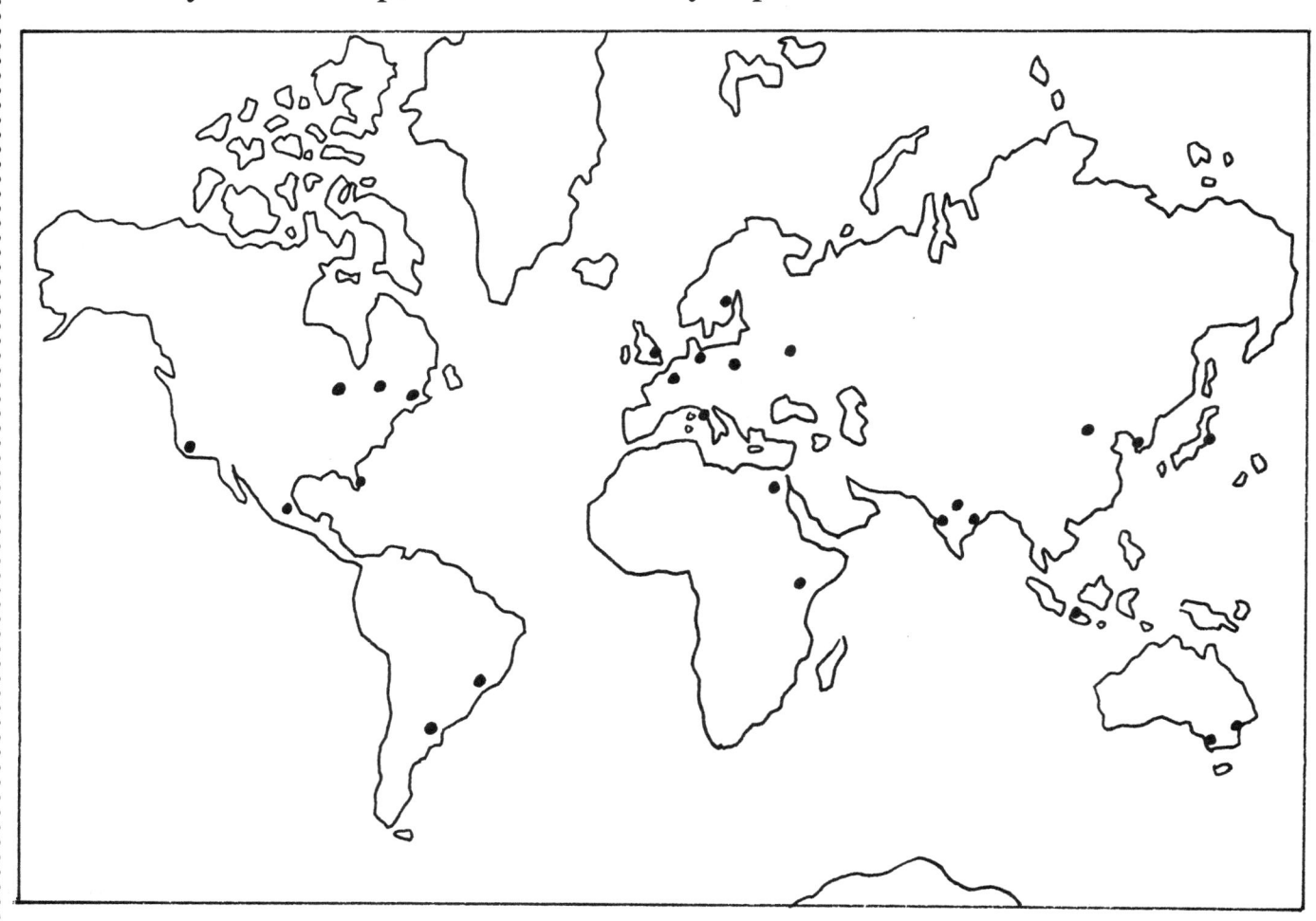

A. New York	**G.** Seoul	**M.** Nairobi	**S.** Buenos Aires	**Y.** Berlin
B. Cairo	**H.** Calcutta	**N.** Paris	**T.** Bombay	**Z.** New Delhi
C. Moscow	**I.** Miami	**O.** Tokyo	**U.** Beijing	
D. Rome	**J.** Toronto	**P.** Los Angeles	**V.** Jakarta	
E. Rio de Janeiro	**K.** Sydney	**Q.** Quebec	**W.** Mexico City	
F. Melbourne	**L.** Copenhagen	**R.** London	**X.** Stockholm	

© 1996 Troll Creative Teacher Ideas

Capital Concentration

Play a "capital cities" version of the game *Concentration* with students, using capital cities from around the world. Begin by writing the name of a capital city on a 3" x 5" index card. Then write the name of the country that city is the capital of on another index card. (For example, you might write *Paris* on one card and *France* on another.)

Continue filling out index cards until 20 to 30 pairs have been completed. Some suggested pairs are:

Australia	Canberra
Belgium	Brussels
Benin	Porto-Novo
Brazil	Brasilia
Canada	Ottawa
Chile	Santiago
China	Beijing
Cuba	Havana
Ecuador	Quito
Ethiopia	Addis Ababa
Finland	Helsinki
Greece	Athens
Iceland	Reykjavik
Indonesia	Jakarta
Ireland	Dublin
Israel	Jerusalem
Kenya	Nairobi
North Korea	Pyongyang
South Korea	Seoul
Lithuania	Vilnius
Netherlands	Amsterdam
Norway	Oslo
Pakistan	Islamabad
Philippines	Quezon City
Poland	Warsaw
Saudi Arabia	Riyadh
Spain	Madrid
Ukraine	Kiev
U.S.A.	Washington, D.C.
Venezuela	Caracas
Zaire	Kinshasa

Shuffle the cards and let two students at a time play the game. Lay the cards out facedown on the floor or a table.

Have the first player turn over two random cards. If the cards are a match (a capital city and its country), the player may keep the cards. If not, the next player goes.

Play continues until all the pairs have been matched. The player with the most matches wins.

Store the cards in a large envelope. Encourage children to play the game during free time.

Current Happenings

During a study unit about current events, ask each student to select an important world city to research. Have each child look for articles about the selected city in newspapers and weekly news magazines. Encourage students to watch the news on television each night to find out any current news stories that concern the selected city. Students may also wish to contact travel agencies to see if there are any brochures about their cities.

After several weeks, ask each student to organize the information he or she has gathered to make a book about the selected city. Ask each child to be sure to include an introduction giving important information about the city, such as location, population, climate, and industry. Then tell students to give brief histories of their cities before discussing what is currently happening.

Have students make covers for their books. Encourage students to give their books titles reflecting the current events taking place.

Punch three holes along the left side of the gathered pages of each book. Tie yarn through each hole to bind the pages together. Then ask volunteers to share their findings with the rest of the class. Place all the books in the social studies center for everyone to review.

As a follow-up, ask each student to write a story about what he or she thinks it would be like to live in the selected city. Attach these stories to a bulletin board under the title of "Life in a Great City."

Let's Play "Geography"!

The traditional car game "Geography" is an excellent way to stimulate students to think of and remember the names of various places and regions. The game may be played either with the entire class or with small groups of four or five students each.

To begin the game, call out the name of the town in which your school is located. Then ask the first player to name a place that begins with the last letter of the town's name. For example, if the name of the town is "Greenville," the first player would need to think of a place with a name that begins with an *E*.

Play continues with each player naming a country, city, or town that begins with the last letter of the place named in the previous player's turn. If desired, eliminate players if they are unable to think of places beginning with the appropriate letters. Then the last player remaining is the winner. Or simply use the game as a review tool and have students help their classmates think of answers when necessary.

You may wish to have students play the game again after a short period of time has passed by. Encourage students to look through atlases and other reference books to learn the names of more places before the next game of "Geography." Variations of this game may also be played with the names of rivers, mountains, deserts, and other physical features or by limiting the answers to cities, towns, and counties within your state.

Population Scramble

Name _____

Unscramble the name of each city below. Then write a number from 1 to 10 next to each city, placing 1 next to the city with the largest population and 10 next to the city with the smallest population. Use an atlas or encyclopedia if you need help!

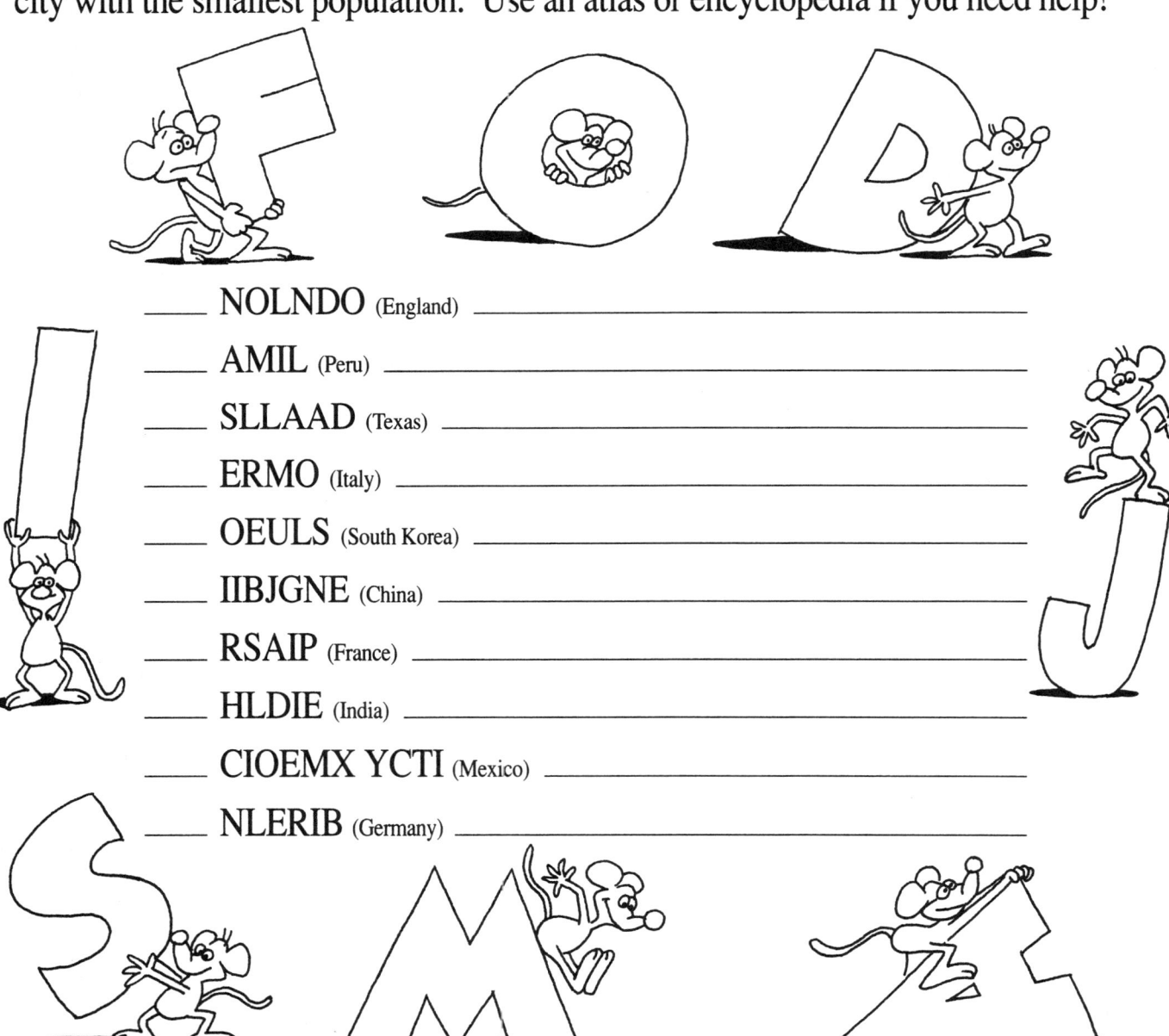

___ NOLNDO (England) _____

___ AMIL (Peru) _____

___ SLLAAD (Texas) _____

___ ERMO (Italy) _____

___ OEULS (South Korea) _____

___ IIBJGNE (China) _____

___ RSAIP (France) _____

___ HLDIE (India) _____

___ CIOEMX YCTI (Mexico) _____

___ NLERIB (Germany) _____

BONUS: Make a list of ten cities, and have a friend make a list of his or her own. Then exchange papers and try to rank the cities on the lists in order of population!

© 1996 Troll Creative Teacher Ideas

Rivers of the World

Name _____

Look at the map of North America and South America below. Identify the rivers by writing the appropriate number next to the name of each river in the box below. Use an atlas or encyclopedia if you need help!

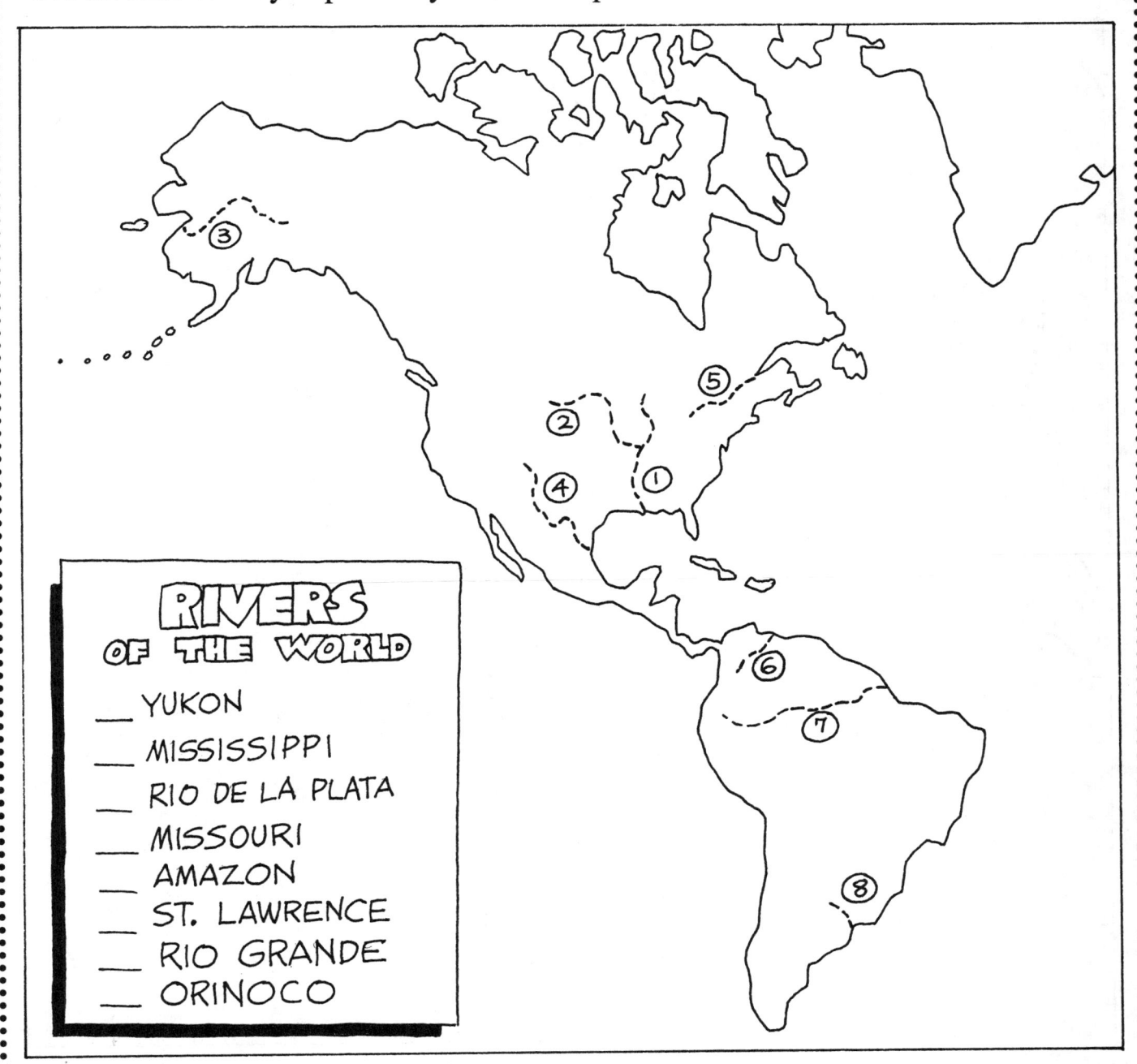

RIVERS OF THE WORLD

___ YUKON
___ MISSISSIPPI
___ RIO DE LA PLATA
___ MISSOURI
___ AMAZON
___ ST. LAWRENCE
___ RIO GRANDE
___ ORINOCO

© 1996 Troll Creative Teacher Ideas

Rivers of the World

Name _____

Look at the map of Europe, Asia, Africa, and Australia below. Identify the rivers by writing the appropriate number next to the name of each river in the box below. Use an atlas or an encyclopedia if you need help!

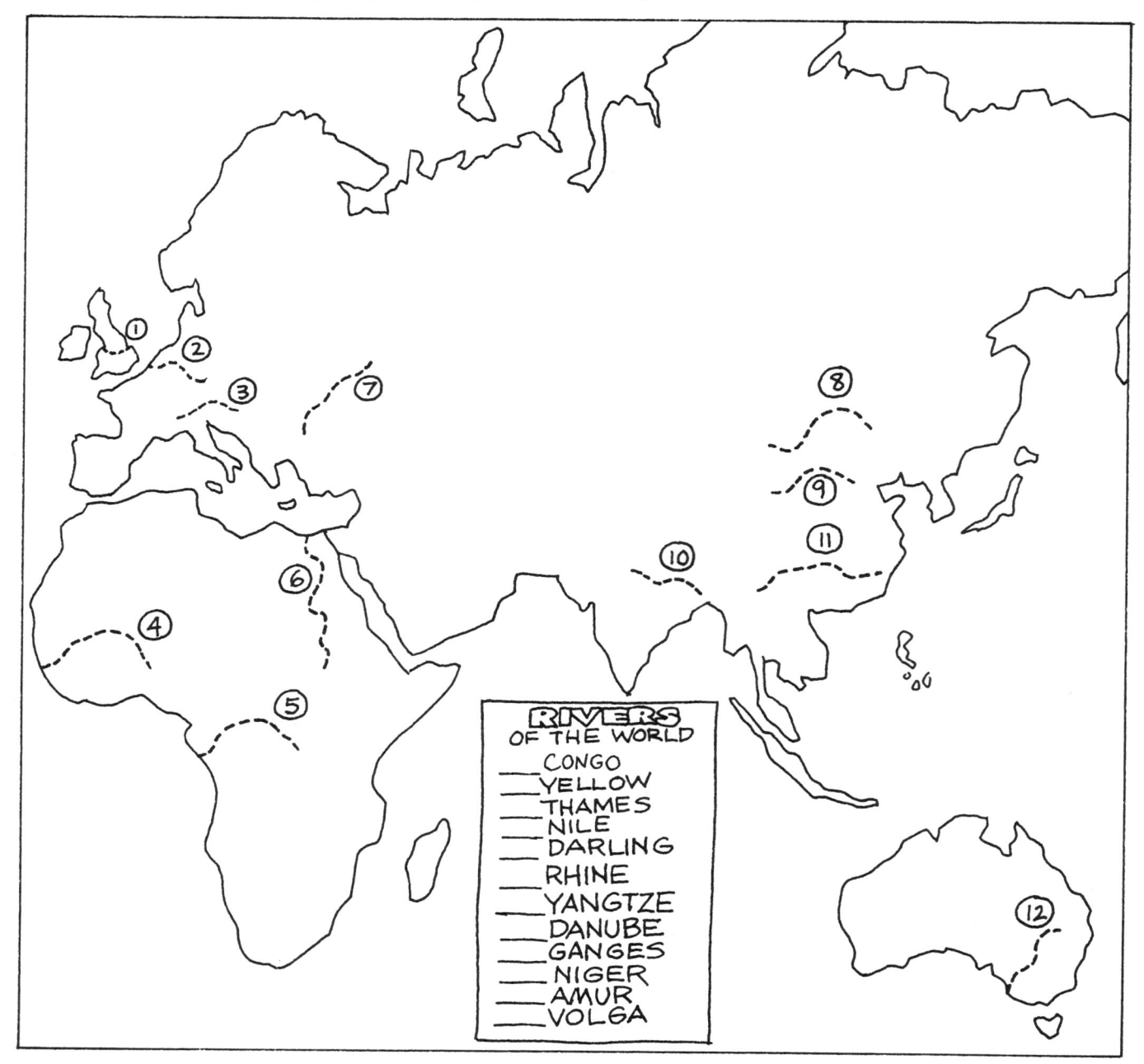

RIVERS OF THE WORLD

___ CONGO
___ YELLOW
___ THAMES
___ NILE
___ DARLING
___ RHINE
___ YANGTZE
___ DANUBE
___ GANGES
___ NIGER
___ AMUR
___ VOLGA

© 1996 Troll Creative Teacher Ideas

Climate Mural Map

MATERIALS:
- masking tape
- mural paper
- markers
- paints and paintbrushes

DIRECTIONS:

1. Have a class discussion about the climates of different areas of the world. Define the various kinds of climate, such as:

Continental—Warm to cool summers; cold winters; moderate precipitation
Highland—High-altitude climate; cooler and wetter than nearby climates
Mediterranean—Hot, dry summers; mild, rainy winters
Equatorial—Hot temperatures; heavy precipitation in season
Tropical—Hot temperatures; heavy precipitation year-round
Desert—Hot to cold temperatures; very little precipitation
Polar—Consistently cold temperatures; very little precipitation

2. Tape together 8' lengths of mural paper to make a mural surface approximately 6' x 8'. Then have the class work together to draw an outline of a world map on the mural.
3. Tell students to use reference books to research the different types of climate on each continent. Then assign a color for each climate that students should represent on their mural map.
4. Let students paint in the areas of the map to show the appropriate climates. Have a small group of students work together to design the title for the map.
5. Attach the mural map to a school hallway for all to see.

Climate Clues

Name _____

Read the clues below. Then write in the name of the type of climate being described.

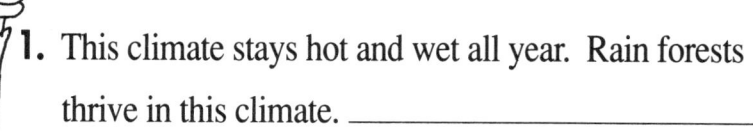

1. This climate stays hot and wet all year. Rain forests thrive in this climate. _____

2. This climate has very high temperatures during the day. At night, however, the temperature may go down to freezing. Very few plants and animals can live in this climate. _____

3. This climate changes, depending on the altitude. In general, the temperatures tend to be a little colder, and precipitation is often heavy. _____

4. This climate has cool to warm summers but cold winters. _____

5. This climate is only found at or near the North and South poles. It has very cold temperatures and little precipitation year-round. _____

© 1996 Troll Creative Teacher Ideas

Wonders of the World

Name _____

On the lines provided, tell where each of these natural wonders is located.

1. K2 (Godwin Austen) _____
2. Sahara Desert _____
3. Grand Canyon _____
4. Great Barrier Reef _____
5. Niagara Falls _____
6. Mount Everest _____
7. Angel Falls _____
8. Lake Baykal _____
9. Kilimanjaro _____
10. Ayers Rock _____

Choose one of the above places to research. Then write a poem about this natural wonder on the lines below.

_____
_____
_____
_____
_____
_____

© 1996 Troll Creative Teacher Ideas

Language Lessons

Name _____

Draw lines to match each country to the language(s) spoken there. If you need help, use an encyclopedia!

1. Wales
2. China
3. India
4. Canada
5. Netherlands
6. Switzerland
7. Norway
8. Egypt
9. Ireland
10. Australia
11. Brazil
12. New Zealand
13. Benin
14. Denmark
15. Argentina

a. Arabic
b. French
c. English and Maori
d. Mandarin
e. Gaelic
f. French and German
g. Welsh
h. Hindi
i. Spanish
j. Portuguese
k. French and English
l. Danish
m. Norwegian
n. English
o. Dutch

© 1996 Troll Creative Teacher Ideas

Changing Currency

Reproduce a current chart of exchange rates from around the world once for each child. Then tell students they will be setting up a class bookstore using money from various countries.

Ask one group of students to price each book using different currencies. For example, one book might cost 6 Swiss francs, while another might cost 2 pounds sterling. (Be sure students are pricing books reasonably and converting the price to dollars as they go.)

Have another group of students make play money for the different currencies being used. Encourage students to use an encyclopedia and other reference books to find out the different denominations of each currency. Provide children with construction paper, oaktag, crayons or markers, and scissors to make the money.

Tell another group of students to be the cashiers for the bookstore. Distribute the play money to a group of shoppers. Have each child choose one or two books to buy using the play money. The cashiers should make change for each purchase using currency from the appropriate country.

When each shopper returns to his or her desk, have that student convert the amount of money spent into dollars using the exchange-rate chart provided.

Rotate the groups of shoppers and cashiers so that everyone has a turn at both jobs. If desired, invite other classes in to "shop" at the worldwide bookstore.

© 1996 Troll Creative Teacher Ideas

Best Books About Geography

Place some or all of the books on the list below in the classroom social studies center when discussing geography. Encourage students to read the books or use them as reference sources.

The Book of Where: Or How to Be Naturally Geographic by Neill Bell (Little, Brown, 1982)

How to Use Maps and Globes by Helen H. Carey (Franklin Watts, 1983)

Lost Cities by Roy A. Gallant (Franklin Watts, 1985)

Maps and Globes by Jack Knowlton (HarperCollins, 1986)

The Wonderful World of Maps by James F. Madden (Hammond, 1977)

Animals Around the World

Name _____

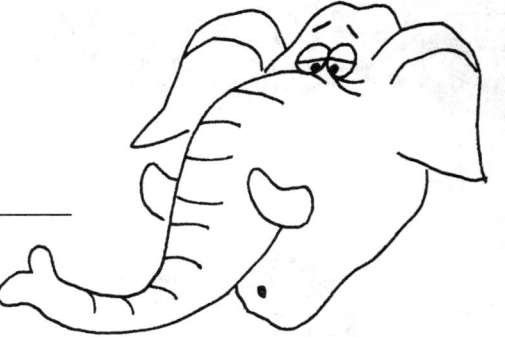

Animals, like people, must adapt to their climates. Read the list of the animals below. Write the name of the place or places where each animal may be found in its natural habitat. Then tell some characteristics of each animal that show that it has adapted to its environment.

1. giraffe _____
_____
_____

2. elk _____
_____
_____

3. gorilla _____
_____
_____

4. panda _____
_____
_____

5. snow leopard _____
_____
_____

6. land iguana _____
_____
_____

7. kangaroo _____
_____
_____

8. elephant _____
_____
_____

9. polar bear _____
_____
_____

10. scorpion _____
_____
_____

11. pit viper _____
_____
_____

12. vicuña _____
_____
_____

© 1996 Troll Creative Teacher Ideas

Class Cookbook

DIRECTIONS:
1. Divide the class into small groups of four students each. Assign each group to research the foods of a particular country or region. For example, ask one group to find out about foods in France and another to find out about foods in India.
2. After each group has learned some basic information about the foods of the assigned country, ask the group to choose a simple recipe from that country to make for the class. Some suggested foods are:

chicken Kiev	tortillas	minestrone
pizza	jambalaya	sauerbraten
pierogi	curried rice	chocolate mousse

3. Give each group an ample amount of time to collect the ingredients and other necessary materials for the recipe. Encourage the groups to let their classmates help with the preparation of the recipe.
4. After the recipe has been made and sampled, ask each group to discuss the foods native to the assigned country and explain why certain kinds of foods are popular in the cuisine of their particular area (for example, curried food in India).

Geographical Homes

Have a class discussion about the different types of homes around the world. Ask students to name some styles of homes they know (such as adobe homes, log homes, apartment houses, houseboats, and so on). Write students' comments on a large piece of oaktag. Add to the list the names of other types of homes with which students may not be familiar, such as thatched-roof homes, chalets, and yurts (domed tents used in parts of Asia). If possible, show pictures of the various homes.

Discuss how homes have traditionally been built to accommodate the climates of particular regions. Talk about the ways in which modern architects keep energy conservation in mind when designing new homes (for example, by using solar panels and placing windows for maximum natural lighting).

Ask each student to pick an area in the world where he or she might like to live. Then have the student research the climate and geographical surroundings of that area to determine what type of home would suit the area best.

Have students draw pictures of the exteriors of their homes and design "bird's-eye view" blueprints of the interiors. Have students tell where their homes are located, and encourage them to explain the critical thinking involved in designing their homes on a separate piece of paper.

Give each student a chance to present his or her home to the rest of the class. Then place the drawings and blueprints on a bulletin board under the title "Dream Homes Around the World."

U.S. Landmarks Game

MATERIALS:
- crayons or markers
- scissors
- glue
- letter-sized file folder
- clear contact paper
- different-colored construction paper
- penny, nickel, dime, quarter (optional)
- envelope
- die

DIRECTIONS:
1. Reproduce the game board on pages 85-86. Color the game board, cut it out, and then mount it on the inside of a letter-sized file folder.
2. Reproduce the game cards on page 87 six times. Color the game cards and mount them on oaktag. On the blank side of each card, write the name of the state in which the landmark is located. Then laminate the cards and cut them apart.
3. Reproduce the "How to Play" instructions on this page once. Cut them out and glue them to the front of the file folder.
4. Make playing pieces by cutting four different-colored circles from construction paper (or use a penny, nickel, dime, and quarter as playing pieces).
5. Glue an envelope to the back of the file folder. Store the game cards and playing pieces inside.

HOW TO PLAY:
(for two to four players)
1. Shuffle the game cards and place them faceup in a pile next to the game board.
2. The youngest player goes first. That player rolls a die and moves the indicated number of spaces on the game board.
3. If a player lands on a "landmark" circle, he or she draws a card from the pile. That player then tries to name the state in which the landmark is located. If he or she is correct, the player may keep the card. If he or she is incorrect, the card is placed on the bottom of the pile.
4. Play continues around the board. If a player draws a landmark card he or she has already collected, the card is placed at the bottom of the pile and the next card is drawn.
5. The player who has the most landmark cards when he or she reaches Finish is the winner.

© 1996 Troll Creative Teacher Ideas

U.S. Landmarks Game

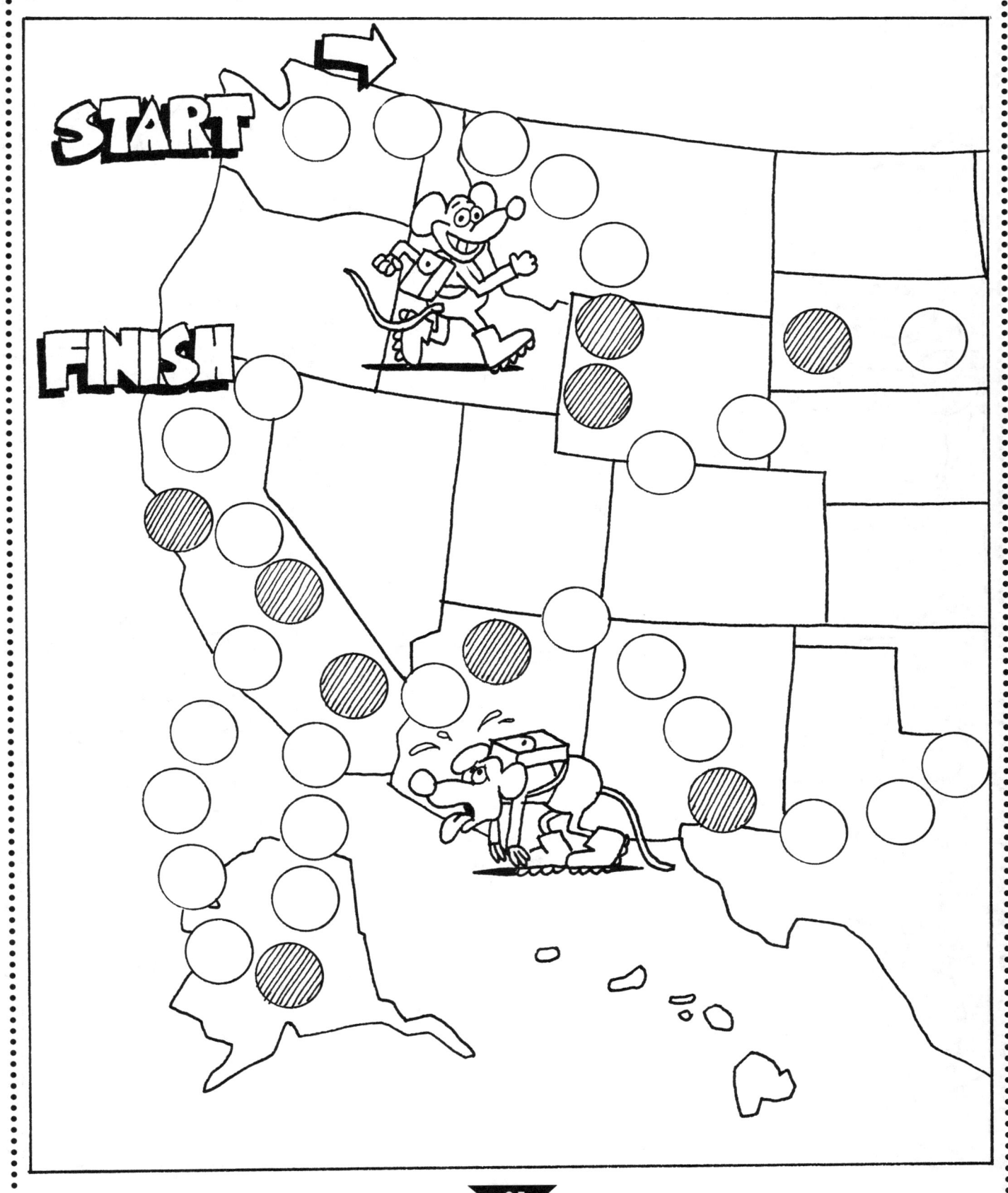

START

FINISH

85
© 1996 Troll Creative Teacher Ideas

U.S. Landmarks Game

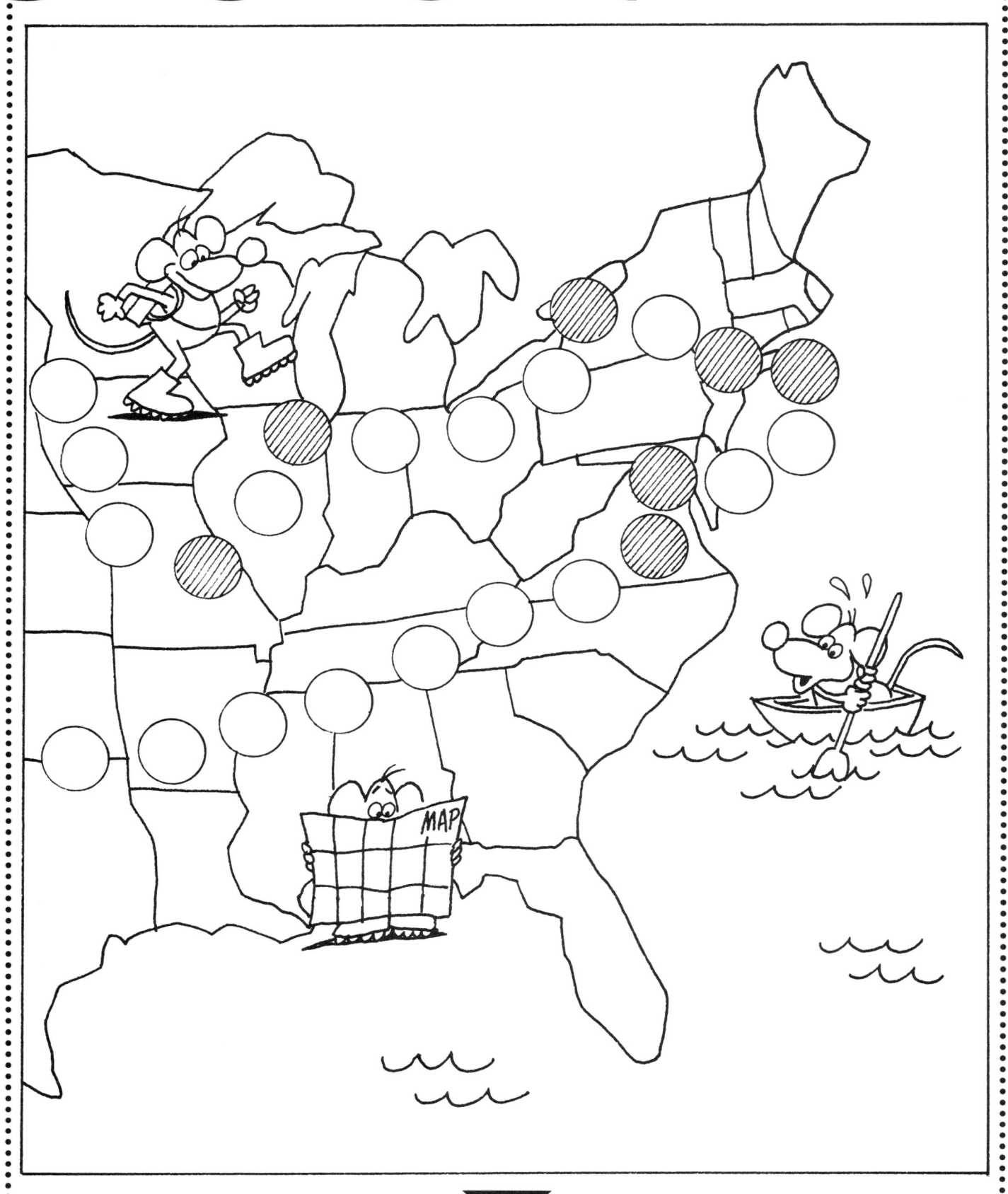

86

U.S. Landmarks Game

STATUE OF LIBERTY	NIAGARA FALLS	MOUNT RUSHMORE	GRAND CANYON
SEQUOIA FOREST	GOLDEN GATE BRIDGE	OLD FAITHFUL	GATEWAY ARCH ST. LOUIS
WHITE HOUSE	EMPIRE STATE BUILDING	MONTICELLO	DENALI
JOSHUA TREE	CARLSBAD CAVERNS	SEARS TOWER	GRAND TETONS

© 1996 Troll Creative Teacher Ideas

Geographical Glossary

Here are some geographical terms to explain and share with the class.

biogeography (ecogeography)   The study of plant and animal distribution on Earth; closely related to ecology.

climatology   The study of weather patterns, climate, and seasonal changes, and how these are shaped; related to meteorology.

cultural geography   The study of the distribution and relationships of cultural groups and traits, such as religion, language, architecture, and place names.

economic geography   The study of the location of economic activities, such as mining, manufacturing, and farming, and the reasons for the selections of locations.

geomorphology   The study of Earth's land forms, including their age and origin.

Geographical Glossary

historical geography   The study of the location of human activities in the past and of how historical events and the natural environment affected these activities.

latitude   The distance north or south of the Equator, as measured on a map or a globe.

longitude   The measured distance east or west of the Prime Meridian at Greenwich, England, as measured on a map or a globe.

political geography   The study of governmental units and political borders; this discipline closely involves historical geography as well.

population geography   The study of the number and distribution of people and of how these patterns change.

topography   The geographical representation of the physical features of an area on a map or a globe.

urban geography   The study of the origin and growth of cities and of the special needs (transportation, sanitation, recreation) within cities.

Answers

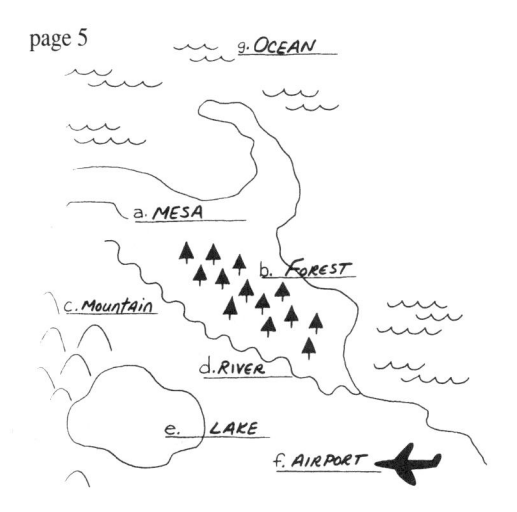

page 5

a. MESA
b. FOREST
c. Mountain
d. RIVER
e. LAKE
f. AIRPORT
g. OCEAN

page 6

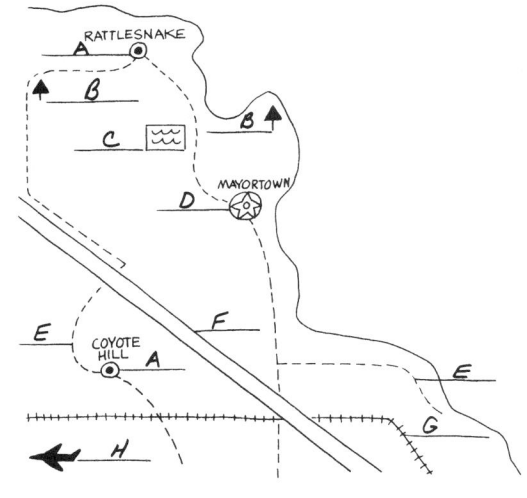

(map with labeled locations: Rattlesnake A, B, C, Mayortown D, Coyote Hill, E, F, A, E, G, H)

page 7
1. southwest
2. Merrimack River
3. Cape Cod
4. west
5. Atlantic Ocean
6. Martha's Vineyard and Nantucket Island
7. There are no deserts in Massachusetts.

page 8
1. Go north on Walnut Avenue until you get to North Avenue. Make a right on North Avenue; then make a left onto Springfield Avenue. Follow Springfield to Kenilworth Boulevard. Nomahegan Park is on Kenilworth.
2. Garwood, Clark, Cranford, and Linden
3. no
4. north
5. in the Northeast corner of Kenilworth
6. Oak Ridge Park in Garwood
7. off Walnut Avenue

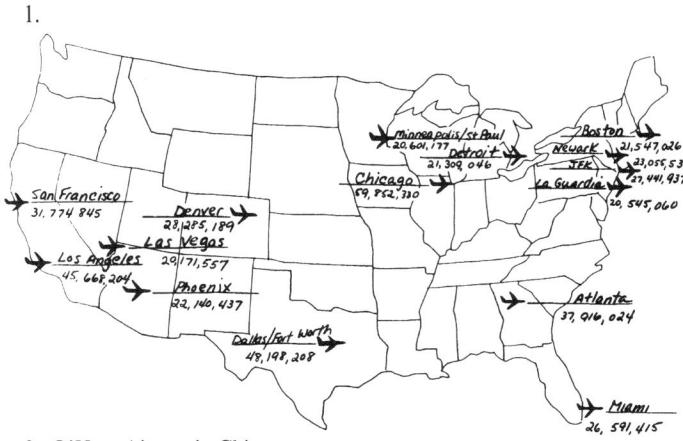

page 9-10
1. (US map with airports labeled)
- San Francisco 31,774,845
- Los Angeles 45,668,204
- Denver 28,285,189
- Las Vegas 20,171,557
- Phoenix 22,140,437
- Dallas/Fort Worth 48,198,208
- Minneapolis/St. Paul 20,601,177
- Detroit 21,309,046
- Chicago 59,852,320
- Boston 21,547,026
- Newark 23,055,537
- JFK 27,441,437
- La Guardia 20,545,060
- Atlanta 37,916,024
- Miami 26,591,415

2. O'Hare Airport in Chicago
3. northwest
4. New York
5. 6,738,163

page 12
1. west
2. east
3. Manitoba
4. Saskatchewan
5. British Columbia
6. southeast

page 13
1. approximately 70 miles
2. no
3. Dublin
4. approximately 35 minutes
5. approximately 17 miles
6. Knock

page 14
Answers will vary. Possible answers include:
1. mountains, telephone lines, cactus, sun, snake, house, fence, garden, road, bird
2. sun, mountains, cactus, garden, snake, bird, bug, adobe mud from which the bricks of the house were made, land
3. car, house, road, telephone wires, clothing, glasses, cup
4. People are wearing shorts, showing that it's warm. Also, the people seem to be living in a desert.
5. northwest
6. The adobe bricks keep the inside of the house cool. Since the house is only one story high, the heat can't rise, so the house stays cooler in the desert heat.

© 1996 Troll Creative Teacher Ideas

Answers

page 15

1. Each sheaf equals 10,000 metric tons of wheat. Each individual stalk equals 1,000 metric tons of wheat.
2. the Soviet Union
3. the Soviet Union produced 76,000 more metric tons of wheat than Canada.
4. the U.S. and France; the Soviet Union
5. one more sheaf
6. approximately 50 percent; approximately 75 percent

page 16

1. the United States; the Netherlands
2. 23.91 quadrillion more Btu's
3. Mexico and the Netherlands
4. Countries that consume more energy may have more people and more industry that those that consume less energy.
5. about half
6. 18.18 quadrillion Btu's; Japan

page 17

page 18

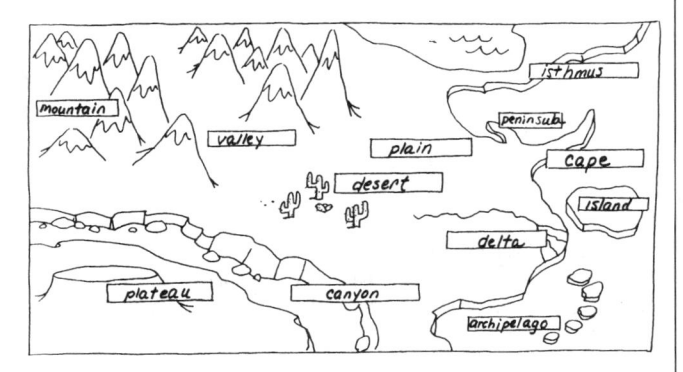

page 20

page 21-22

1. VENEZUELA
2. COLOMBIA
3. GUYANA
4. SURINAME
5. FRENCH GUIANA
6. ECUADOR
7. PERU
8. BRAZIL
9. BOLIVIA
10. CHILE
11. ARGENTINA
12. PARAGUAY
13. URUGUAY

Answers

page 23

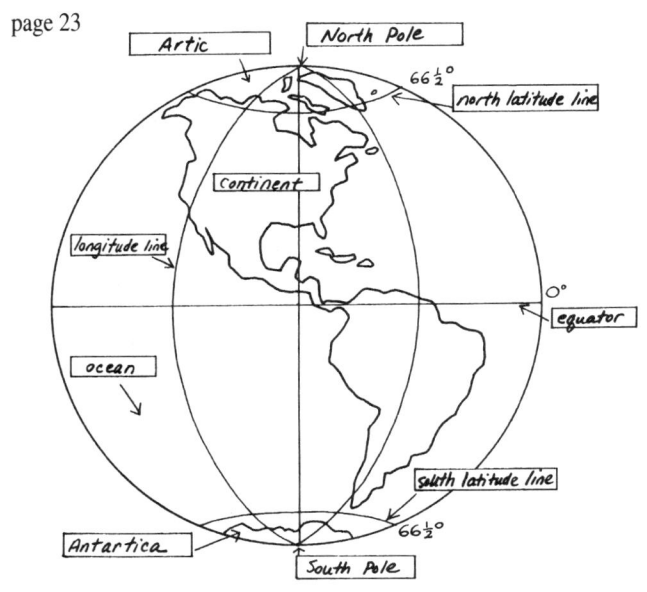

(Globe diagram labeled: Artic, North Pole, north latitude line, 66½°, continent, longitude line, equator, 0°, ocean, south latitude line, 66½°, Antartica, South Pole)

page 24

	Chicago	New York	Houston	Atlanta
Boston	900	200	1550	950
Seattle	1775	2400	1850	2200
Detroit	250	500	1150	600
Philadelphia	700	150	1325	650

page 25

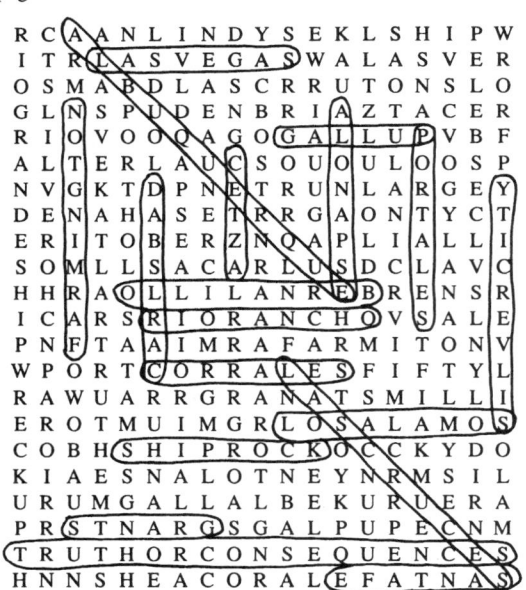

(Word search grid)

These cities and towns can all be found in New Mexico.

page 26

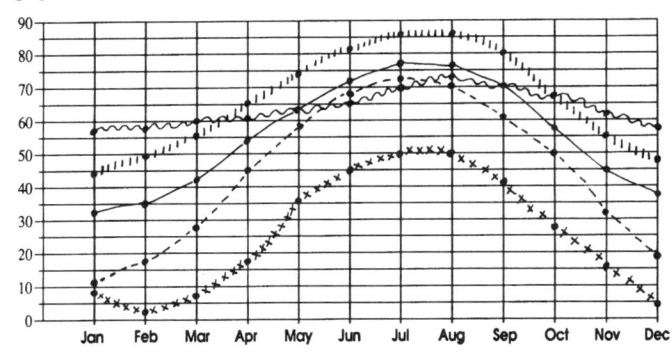

(Line graph with temperatures Jan–Dec, y-axis 0–90)

1. San Diego, CA
2. Dallas/Ft. Worth, TX; Nome, AK
3. Nome, AK
4. Baltimore, MD—coldest: January/warmest: July
   Minneapolis, MN—coldest: January/warmest: July
   Dallas/Ft. Worth, TX—coldest: January/warmest: July & August
   San Diego, CA—coldest: January & December/warmest: August
   Nome, AK—coldest: February/warmest: July

page 27

1. 1903   7. 1953
2. 1908   8. 1968
3. 1909   9. 1970
4. 1911   10. 1974
5. 1912   11. 1986
6. 1916

pages 28-29

(Two pie charts showing world population percentages by continent)

Left chart: Australia 5%, Europe 7%, Antarctica 9%, South America 12%, North America 16%, Africa 21%, Asia 30%

Right chart: Australia 3%, South America 6%, North America 8%, Africa 11%, Europe 24%, Asia 50%

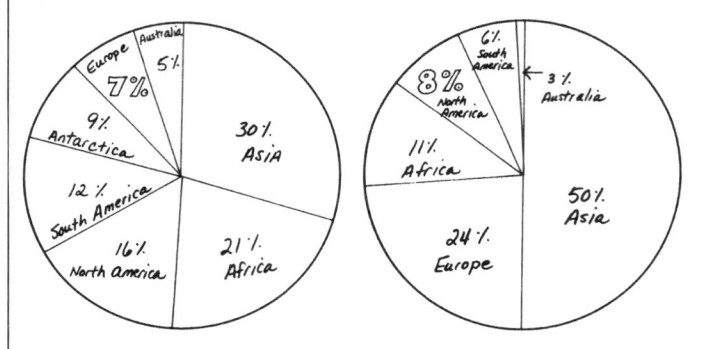

1. Asia
2. Africa and Antarctica
3. Europe has 23.7% more of the world's population than Australia.
4. Because Antarctica has 0% of the world's population.
5. Europe, North America, and South America now have about 38% of the world's population. In the year 2025, Africa may have about 39% of the world's population.

Answers

page 38

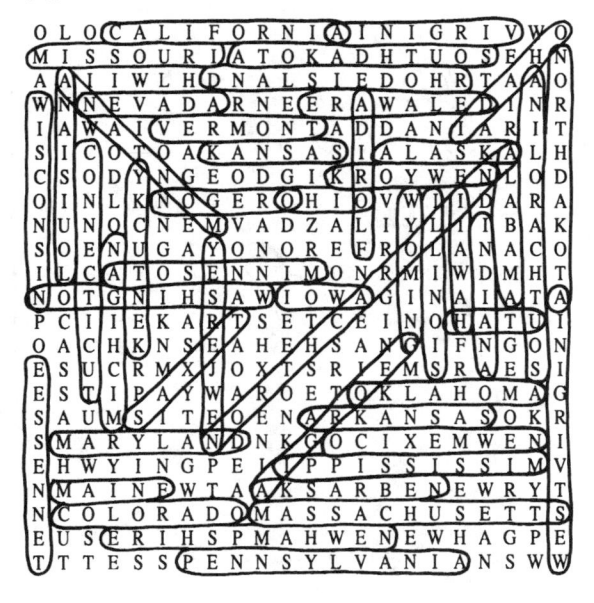

page 45

AZ—Arizona	OK—Oklahoma
CO—Colorado	PA—Pennsylvania
DE—Delaware	RI—Rhode Island
IN—Indiana	SD—South Dakota
KY—Kentucky	TX—Texas
LA—Louisiana	UT—Utah
MD—Maryland	VA—Virginia
NV—Nevada	WY—Wyoming

page 46

Answers will vary. Possible answers include:

Swansea	Daaquam
Europe	Atlanta
Azores	McCloud
Paris	Danube
Acropolis	Innsbruck
Santa Monica	Kauai
Sverdrup	Easter Island
Great Barrier Reef	Minnesota
Uxmal	Elbrus
Lanzhou	Seine
Fitchburg	Amsterdam
Trenton	Rhode Island
Ogemaw	Ottawa
Waterloo	Acapulco
Nantucket	Dakar

page 43

Answers will vary. Possible answers include:
Alaska—cold, wilderness, American
Puerto Rico—warm, sunny, tropical
Australia—dry, warm, large
England—rainy, damp, royal
Siberia—cold, snowy, thinly populated
Switzerland—snowy, neutral, independent
Germany—picturesque, united,
Sahara Desert—hot, dry, oases
South Africa—warm, tropical, dry
Kenya—dry, hot, tropical
Egypt—dry, hot, ancient
China—traditional, beautiful, royal

page 44

page 47

Pie chart:
- Colorado Springs 31%
- Anchorage 30%
- Boston 2%
- Albuquerque 16%
- Little Rock 11%
- Oklahoma 10%

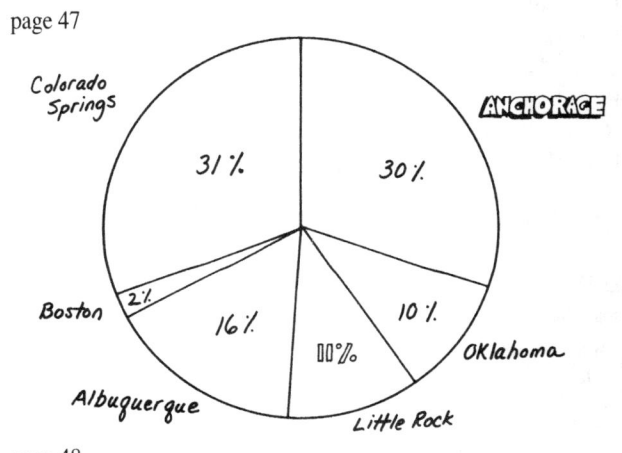

page 48

Answers will vary. Possible answers include:
1. The last sentence is wrong. It could read: Once the magma erupts out of the earth, it piles up and eventually may form a volcanic mountain, or volcano.
2. The last two sentences are wrong. They could read: Dolphins eat mainly fish and squid. Most dolphins have lots of teeth, but they only use them to grasp their food, not to chew it.
3. The fifth sentence is wrong. It could read: The air in the lightning's path gets hot and expands, producing a pressure called thunder.
4. The second sentence is wrong. It could read: Hawaii is a chain of 132 islands in the Pacific Ocean.

© 1996 Troll Creative Teacher Ideas

Answers

page 49

Eat it?	Live in it?	Wear it?
tortilla	hogan	kilt
plantains	flat	turban
mango	palazzo	brogans
poi	pueblo	sari
escargot	yurt	kimono
sushi	villa	veil
	hut	dirndl
		sarong

page 51

1. b
2. e
3. f
4. g
5. k
6. d
7. l
8. c
9. j
10. a
11. h
12. i

page 52

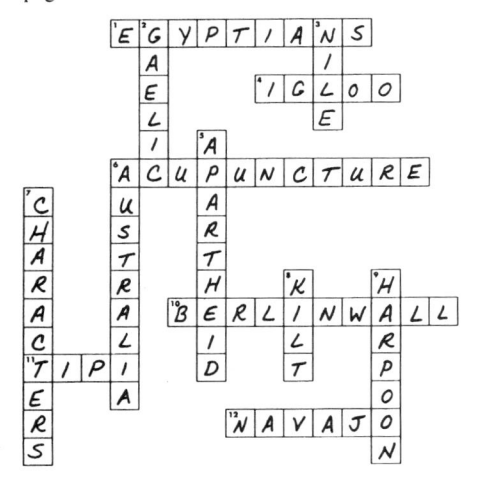

Crossword answers: EGYPTIANS, IGLOO, ACUPUNCTURE, BERLINWALL, NAVAJO, CHARACTERS, TIPI, AUSTRALIA, AZTEC (ARTH...), KILT, HARPOON, NILE, AE(L)I, SARI

page 57

1. Nevada
2. Lima (capital of Peru)
3. Andes
4. Oslo, Norway
5. Black Sea
6. Taiwan
7. Lake Victoria (in East Africa)
8. Bay of Bengal

page 58

Answers will vary.

page 59

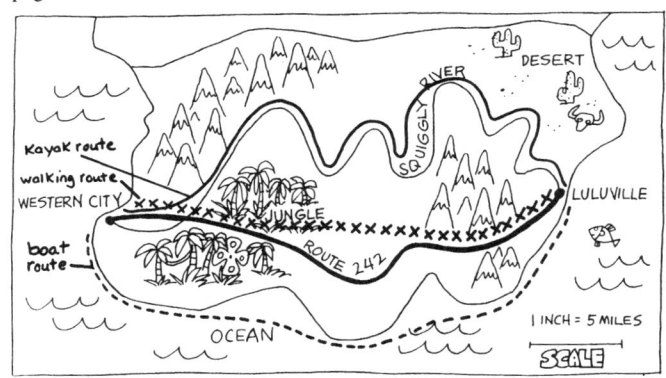

Answers to questions will vary.

page 60

Answers will vary. Possible answers include:

English—United States, Australia, Canada, Great Britain, Ireland, New Zealand, South Africa, Bangladesh, India, Pakistan
Spanish—Spain, Latin America, Puerto Rico, United States
Portuguese—Portugal, Brazil, Mozambique, Angola, United States
Russian—Russia, Georgia, Uzbekistan, Kazakhstan, and all the other countries formerly part of the Soviet Union
Mandarin—China
Japanese—Japan, Korea, Taiwan, Ryukyu islands, Bonin island
Hindi—India
Arabic—Egypt, Iraq, Jordan, Lebanon, Saudi Arabia, Syria, Tunisia
Farsi—Iran
Tagalog—Philippines
Swahili—East Africa (for example, Kenya and Tanzania)
Siouan—United States

page 63

1776
1803
Answers for the second part of this exercise will vary.

page 64

1. Pete's Peak
2. 100 feet
3. 400 feet
4. Mount Rushless
5. Sandy River

Answers

page 61

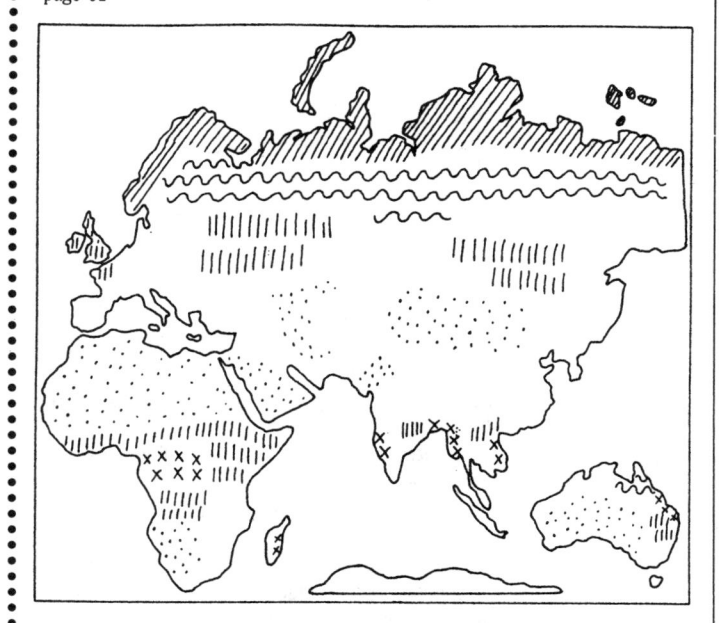

page 62

page 65

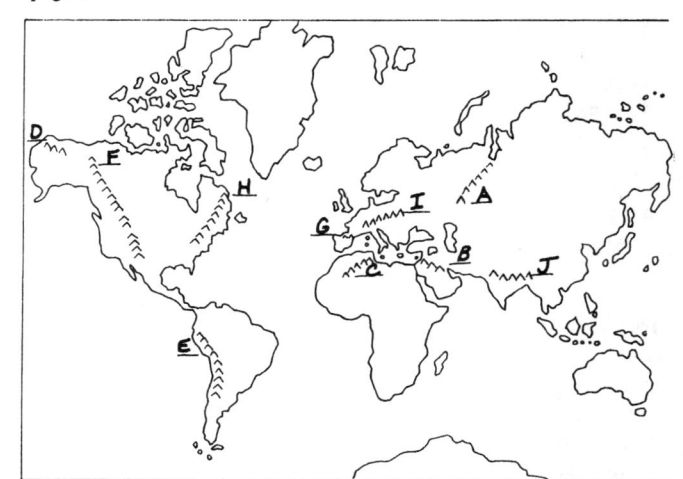

pages 66-67

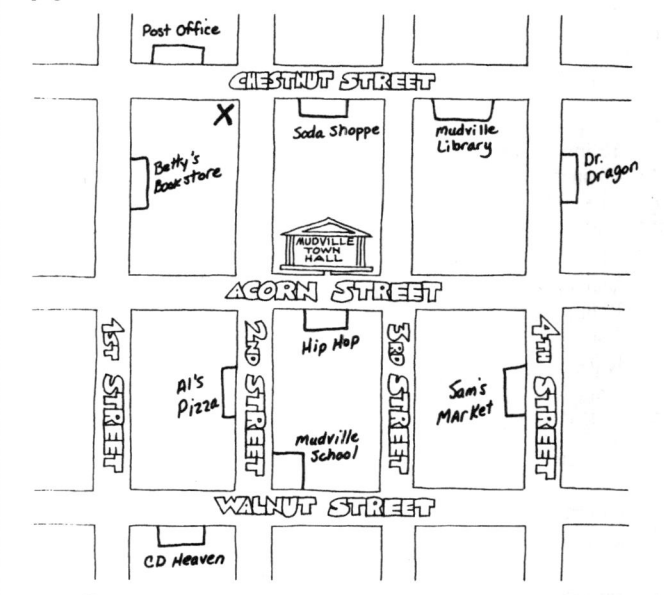

page 68

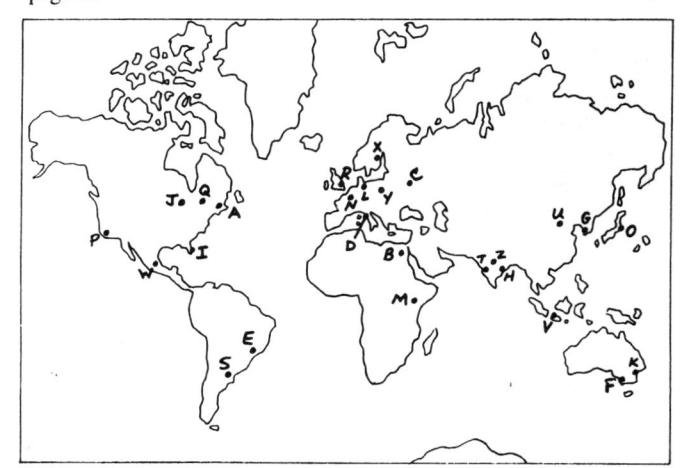

Answers

page 72

<u>3</u> London
<u>6</u> Lima
<u>10</u> Dallas
<u>8</u> Rome
<u>2</u> Seoul
<u>7</u> Beijing
<u>5</u> Paris
<u>4</u> Delhi
<u>1</u> Mexico City
<u>9</u> Berlin

page 73

<u>3</u> Yukon
<u>1</u> Mississippi
<u>8</u> Rio DeLa Plata
<u>2</u> Missouri
<u>7</u> Amazon
<u>5</u> St. Lawrence
<u>4</u> Rio Grande
<u>6</u> Orinoco

page 74

<u>5</u> Congo
<u>9</u> Yellow
<u>1</u> Thames
<u>6</u> Nile
<u>12</u> Darling
<u>2</u> Rhine
<u>11</u> Yangtze
<u>3</u> Danube
<u>10</u> Ganges
<u>4</u> Niger
<u>8</u> Amur
<u>7</u> Volga

page 76

1. tropical
2. desert
3. highland
4. continental
5. polar

page 77

1. China/Kashmir border
2. North Africa
3. United States
4. Australia
5. United States/Canada border
6. Tibet/Nepal
7. Venezuela
8. Siberia
9. East Africa
10. Australia

page 78

1. g
2. d
3. h
4. k
5. o
6. f
7. m
8. a
9. e
10. n
11. j
12. c
13. b
14. l
15. i

page 81

Answers will vary. Possible answers include:

1. giraffe—Africa. The long black hairs at the end of a giraffe's tail are effective for swatting away the tsetse fly.
2. elk—North America, northern Europe. Changes its diet to adapt to seasonal availability of food.
3. gorilla—central Africa. Regularly moves to different feeding sites so all the food supply in one place is not exhausted.
4. panda—China. Eats mostly bamboo shoots, which are plentiful in its natural habitat.
5. snow leopard—Himalaya mountains. Its coat is thin in summer and thick in winter to adapt to climate changes.
6. land iguana—Galapagos islands. The land iguana never goes near water, so it only eats land plants, such as cactuses.
7. kangaroo—Australia. The female has a pouch on its belly to carry its babies. The pouch also has milk glands to feed the babies.
8. elephant—Africa or southern Asia. Since it has no sweat glands, the elephant uses its trunk to spray itself with water to keep cool.
9. polar bear—Antarctica. It is protected from the cold by thick fur that covers everything except the nose and foot pads, plus a thick layer of fat under the skin.
10. scorpion—parts of the United States, tropical countries. Scorpions sleep during the day and are awake at night to hunt their prey, insects and spiders.
11. pit viper—America, East Indies, Asia, parts of Europe. A pit viper's fangs are hollow to carry its poisonous venom to its prey.
12. vicuña—Andes mountains. Since it lives high up in the mountains, the vicuña has year-round feeding and sleeping territories.